D0433760

THIS SHAKING EARTH

GOLDBERG BOWEN & CO

THIS SHAKING EARTH

JOHN GRIBBIN

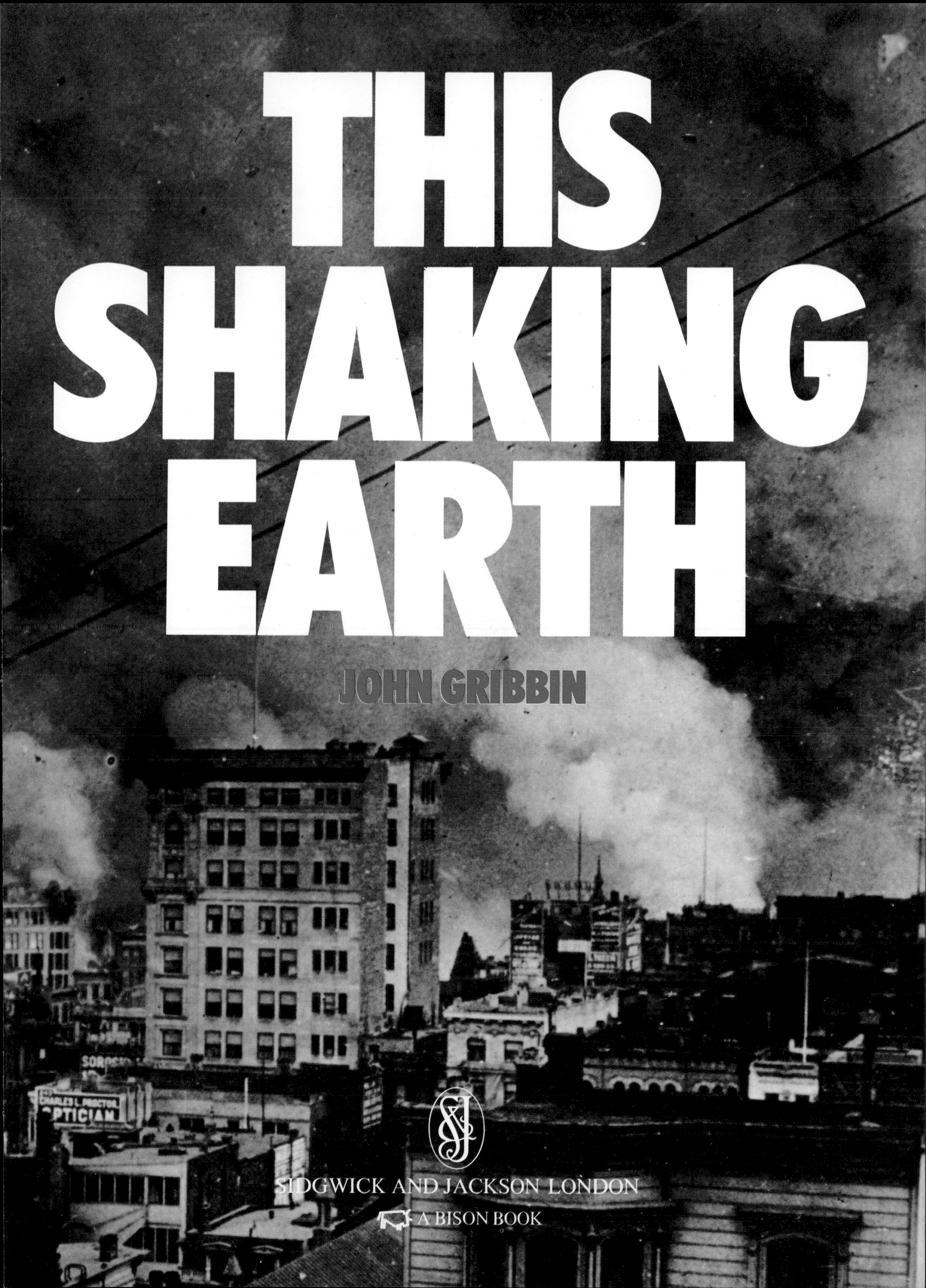

SIDGWICK AND JACKSON LONDON

A BISON BOOK

First published in Great Britain
in 1978 by
Sidgwick and Jackson Limited

ISBN 0 283 98462 7

Printed in Hong Kong

Editor
John Man

Design
Laurence Bradbury

Picture Research
US/Jane Sugden
UK/Annie Horton

Editorial Co-ordinator
Fleur Walsh

Diagrams
Gary Hinks

CONTENTS

1: THE FEEL OF CATASTROPHE
6
2: CRUST AND CRUMBLE
28
3: THE GREAT QUAKES
56
4: ANATOMY OF THE VOLCANO
98
5: THE GREAT ERUPTIONS
130
6: THE FUTURE SHOCKS
170
INDEX
190

1: THE FEEL OF CATASTROPHE

A selection of eyewitness accounts that dramatize the impact of earthquakes and volcanoes on individuals and society.

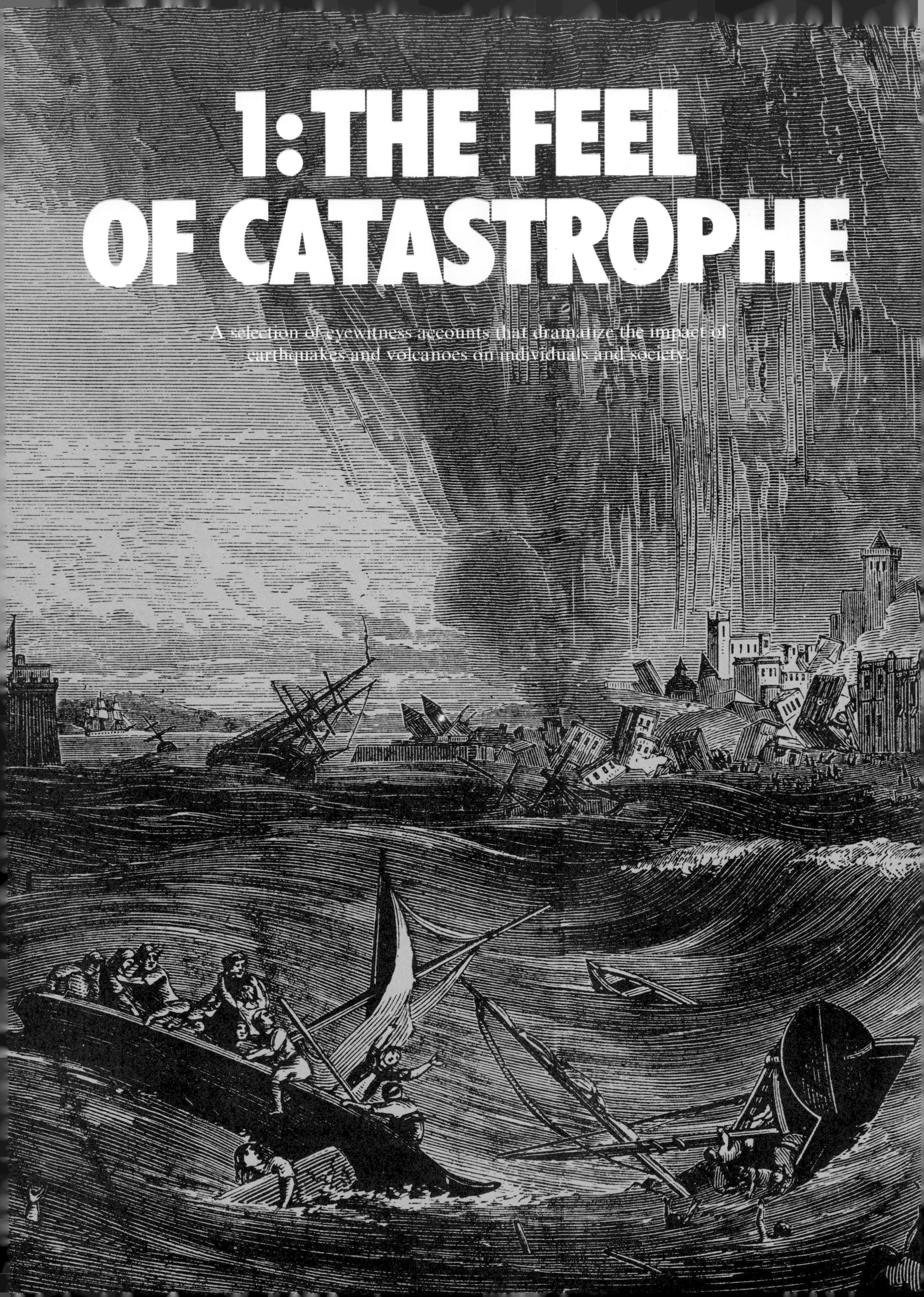

Lisbon crumbles in 1755 under the combined onslaught of an earthquake and a tidal wave.

In *c*. 1450 BC the volcano Thera in the eastern Mediterranean exploded with a violence that contributed to the destruction of the Minoan civilization on Crete and created the legend of Lost Atlantis. In 1976 a devastating earthquake smashed through China, killing more than half a million people and completely destroyed a major city. Across a span of 3500 years in time and 6000 miles these two extreme events dramatize the activity of our proverbially 'solid' Earth. To most people it is indeed solid. But to many millions down through the ages, it has proved to be no such thing. To them, the discovery has been shattering, emotionally, physically and socially. We shall let some of their experiences act as reminders of the impact of such disasters, for there is no more powerful justification for the current scientific drive to understand and control the massive forces the earth so often unleashes.

There are no eyewitness accounts of the destruction of Thera, back in the dawn of our civilization. But accounts do exist of the events in China in 1976 and where better to start than with a look at the most devastating recent earthquake in the world's most heavily populated country?

Earthquake tremors are fairly common in China. But the events of 28 July 1976 were something else. The city of Tangshan was so completely destroyed – with half a million deaths – that visitors almost a year later reported the scene as 'like Hiroshima after the atom bomb . . . a desert of rubble as far as the eye can see across what used to be a city of one million people.' With hundreds of thousands also dead in the region around the city proper, the disaster may well have been the greatest in human history, exceeding the 800,000 reported dead in an earthquake that struck China's Shansi province in 1556.

In the 1976 case, the disaster was made worse by man. Tangshan had been built over some of the richest coal seams in China, and the ground below the city resembled a Gruyère cheese bored through by many shafts and tunnels. When the Earth shook, these cavities collapsed, dropping an entire hospital into one pit and a train into another. The city will be rebuilt – on a new site away from the coalmine.

The eyewitness accounts from Tangshan, the center of destruction, are all from west-

ern observers who reached the scene many months later. A blanket of official secrecy surrounds the events in Tangshan on 28 July 1976, and the reports filtering out of China predominantly come from foreigners in Peking 100 miles away, where the quake was alarming enough. *Daily Telegraph* staff man, Nigel Wade, described the impact of the quake on Peking:

'. . . the room was shaking.

Six floors of flats below us and three above were heaving and rattling, lurching and grinding as a deep rumbling rose to a crescendo all around. Nightmare had become reality.'

A population used to earthquakes may not panic in such disasters, but they also know just what to expect and lose no time in getting out of doors. A foreign student, less used to such events, jumped from a fourth floor window and had to have a leg amputated from the injuries sustained. The normally prudish (by Western standards) Chinese did not always bother to dress fully before hurrying into the streets; and no one went back indoors once he reached safety. The official version of events tells of people remaining calm and displaying 'iron fortitude in dealing with the calamity' and says that 'the revolutionary calm and order displayed by the Peking people in the anti-quake struggle shows to the full the superiority of the socialist system.' But later revelations hint that problems with the socialist system at the time may not have helped the people affected.

It is certainly true, as many Western observers reported, that there was no panic, and the disaster, once it had occurred, was dealt with efficiently. But only a year before the Chinese had achieved remarkable success in predicting a major earthquake – so why did they fail this time? One answer is that some earthquakes are easier to forecast than others, and even so the art of earthquake prediction is still in its first tentative stages of development. But some time after the event the monthly magazine *China Reconstructs* cast a new light on the situation.

At the time of the July disaster China was, politically, in a turmoil. Chairman Mao was ailing and his would-be successors struggled for power. According to *China Reconstructs*, many seismological observatories reported signs that a quake was imminent and attempted to call an emergency conference – but the

VULCAN'S SEAT

Vulcano, the southernmost of the Lipari Islands, just north of Sicily, is named after Vulcan, the ancient god of fire and metalworkers. Though in recent centuries upstaged by its neighbors Etna, Vesuvius and Stromboli, Vulcano in ancient times presented more impressive spectacles than the other three. The local inhabitants, glancing uneasily across from the mainland, must often have imagined they could hear the thunderous rumblings of Vulcan's hammer and anvil, and see the smoke and fire of the fire-god's mighty forge.

Undeterred by the fearsome mythological associations of the mountain's name, Italians have built a modern town in its very shadow. Although the last large-scale eruption was in 1888–90, Vulcano is still active as what is known as a solfatara (from the Italian *solfo*, meaning sulphur), regularly emitting stifling clouds of volcanic gas and steam. One day, it could explode again with a force sufficient to justify its name – the origin of the very word volcano.

A dramatic reconstruction of the earthquake.

Lisbon's St. Nicholas Church after the quake

LISBON'S DEVASTATION

The earthquake in Lisbon in 1755 was perhaps the most shattering – both physically and intellectually – that Europe has ever experienced in recent centuries. Minor shocks were noted all over Europe, and the earthquake which killed an estimated 60,000 people, effectively destroyed a widespread and reassuring philosophical belief in an all-beneficent Deity. The French philosopher and writer, Voltaire, in his biting novel *Candide*, used the earthquake to satirize the view that this is 'the best of all possible worlds' with a deliberately off-hand sketch of the disaster: 'The houses tottered, and their roofs fell to the foundations, and the foundations were scattered; 30,000 inhabitants of all ages and sexes were crushed to death in the ruins.' Eyewitness accounts of the events are rare. The following account is by Thomas Chase, an Englishman who was born in Lisbon, survived the devastating earthquake and died in Bromley, Kent in 1788.

'I was alone in my bed-chamber, four stories from the ground, opening a bureau; when a shaking or trembling of the ground, which I knew immediately to be an earthquake, gentle at first but gradually increasing to greater violence, alarmed me so much, that, turning round to look at the windows, the glass seemed to be falling out . . . I ran directly up into . . . a single room at the top of the house . . . I was no sooner up the stairs, than a prospect the most horrid that imagination can form, appeared before my eyes. The house began to heave to that degree, that, to prevent my being thrown down, I was obliged to put my arm out of a window, and support myself by the wall. Every stone in the walls separating each from the other, and grinding, as did all the walls of the other houses, one against another, with a variety of different motions, made the most dreadful jumbling noise that ears ever heard. . . . I had resolved to throw myself upon the floor, but suppose I did not; for immediately I felt myself falling.' [Chase had actually been thrown out of the window, a fall that injured him severely. He nevertheless made his way clear of the rubble and was looked after by a German merchant, John Forg.]

'It would be impossible to pretend justly to describe the universal horror and distress which every where took place. Many saved themselves by going upon the water, whilst others found there the death which they hoped to have avoided. Some were wonderfully preserved by getting upon the tops of houses; and more were equally so by retiring to the bottoms of them. Others again were unhurt, but imprisoned beneath the ruin of their dwellings, to be soon burnt alive! while the Dutchmen in particular were said to have escaped by the fire's coming to the ruins of their houses, and lighting them through passages, which otherwise they would never have found out. In short, Death in every shape soon grew familiar to the eye! The earnest, but neglected, supplications of the maimed, no less than the violent and vociferous prayers of persons who thought it to be the day of judgment, added unspeakably to the general distraction. The river is said in a most wonderful manner to have risen and fallen several times successively; at one time threatening to overwhelm the lower parts of the city; and directly afterwards leaving the ships almost aground, shewing rocks that never had been seen before . . .

The duration of the first shock, which came on without any warning, except a great noise heard by the people near the water-side, is variously reported, but by none as less than three minutes and a half. At the close of which, as I imagine, it was when I was thrown over the wall and fell about *four stories* down, between the houses! . . . Three times I thought myself inevitably lost; the *first*, when I beheld all the city moving like the undulations of water; the *second*, when I found myself shut up between four walls, and the *third* time, when, with that vast conflagration before my eyes, I considered myself as deserted, in Mr Forg's house; and even in the Square, where I remained all Saturday night and Sunday, when the almost continual trembling of the earth, as well as the sinking of the great stone quay adjoining to this Square, at the third great shock about twelve o'clock, the quay being then, as it was said, covered with three thousand people, all endeavouring to get into boats and were swallowed up, boats and all, which was the reason why so few boats ventured upon the river for some time after: all this made me fearful lest the waters had undermined the Square, and that, at every succeeding convulsion, we should sink; or else, as the ground was low, and even with the water, that the least rising of it would overflow us. Full of these terrors, as well as tortured by the distresses already mentioned, it more than once occurred to me, that the Inquisition, with all its utmost cruelty, could not have invented half such a variety of tortures for the mind as we were then suffering.'

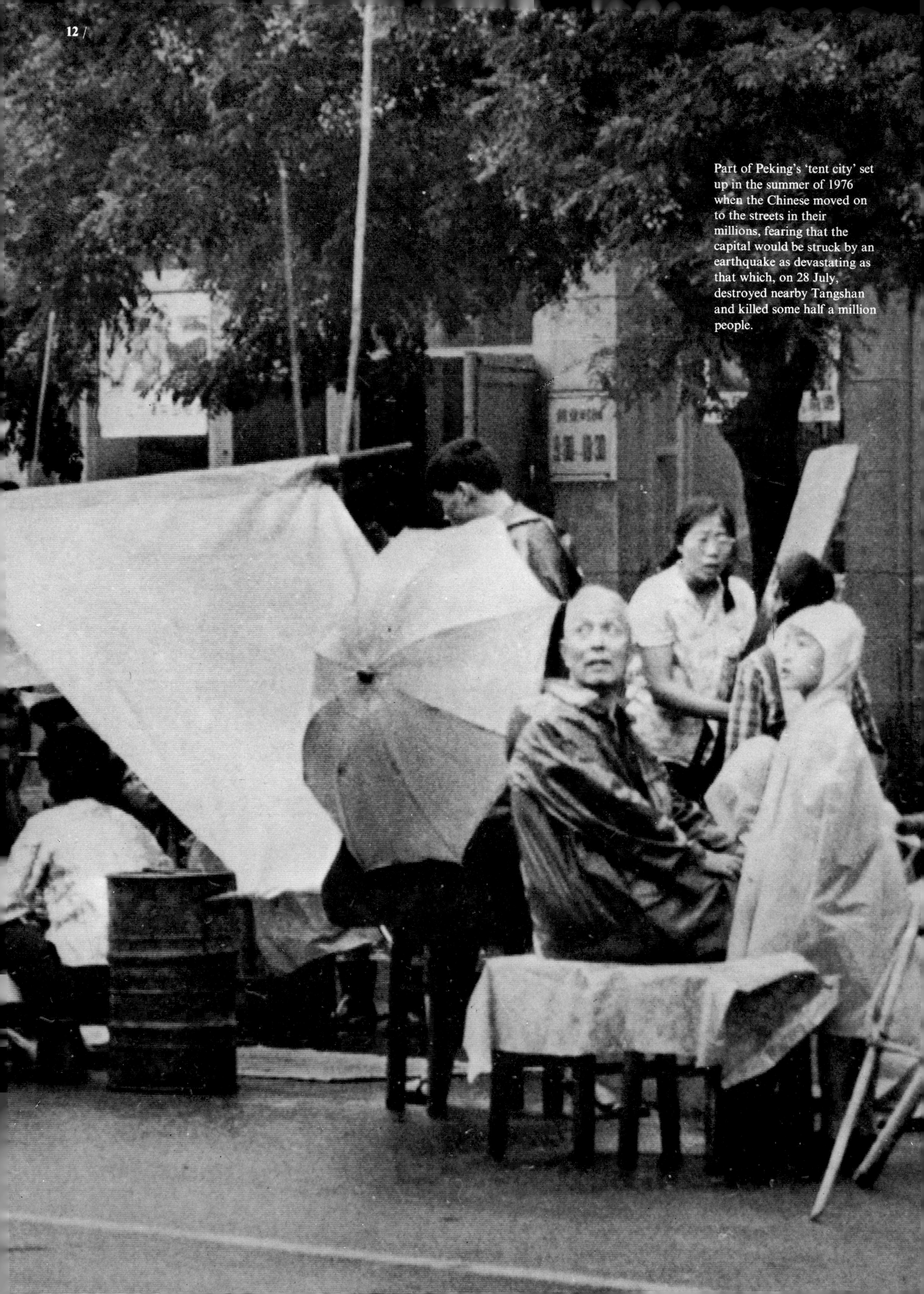

Part of Peking's 'tent city' set up in the summer of 1976 when the Chinese moved on to the streets in their millions, fearing that the capital would be struck by an earthquake as devastating as that which, on 28 July, destroyed nearby Tangshan and killed some half a million people.

group now known as the 'gang of four' was too busy rooting out political opponents, disrupting every aspect of life including the scientific study of earthquakes. The conference was never held, warnings were never issued, and according to the present regime the 'gang of four' must take the blame.

Following the first quake, millions of Chinese lived outside in tents until the hazard from secondary tremors had passed; now, rather belatedly, official warnings of more to come were issued. The warnings encouraged disciplined action, and not just among the Chinese, as Wade's story goes on to reveal: 'the soot-blackened faces of staff burning secret documents . . . were evidence enough for me that at the British Embassy the quake threat is taken as real'.

Even in disciplined Peking, however, there was some looting. Described in official terms as 'sabotage by class enemies,' such activity seems to go grimly hand in hand with any great natural disaster.

What do witnesses of other disasters have to tell about their feelings when the Earth moves? A survivor of the Tokyo earthquake of 1 September 1923 said:

'The shock apparently came from directly underneath and kept us bouncing . . . . The sound was a series of dull thumps very similar to that of a series of heavy charges of dynamite being exploded at some depth . . . a tidal wave, if it could be called such. No wave appeared, but the water rose very rapidly. Very large boulders and large pine trees were tossed about like peas in a boiling pot.'

From Agadir, in Morocco, 29 February 1960: 'Survivors . . . were in complete agreement as to the sudden, sharp, and brief nature of the ground motions. Many stated that the ground gave a sudden lurch, that it was "kicked out from under their feet." '

And what of volcanoes, the other outward aspect of the violence of the shaking Earth? The events at Sakurajima, Japan, in 1914 highlighted the links between earthquakes

and volcanoes, and the value of predictions of disaster. The Sakurajima eruption was forecast precisely because of a series of preceding earthquakes; with the citizenry forewarned, there was very little loss of life when the volcano erupted on 12 January. Everyone is familiar, these days, with TV films of volcanoes producing lava which flows like a red hot river down a mountainside. But far less appreciated is the explosiveness of many volcanic outbursts. On this occasion, 'American teachers . . . testified that their ears were aching as a result of the incessant detonations and the everlasting rattling of the paper partitions of the houses'.

And one of those American teachers described the climax of the eruption in a letter home: 'On the evening of the 13th, skyrockets of scoria shot from the crater in all directions . . . a tremendous force sent a fountain of fire more than 6000 feet into the air. Then this incredible column fell, and from an incredible height tumbled like a vast Niagara of fire in wide streams onto the island and into the water . . . sparkling cascades of fire [flowed] toward the sea . . . lava streams rushed like molten iron into ravines, filling them, solidifying and piling up in fields of enormous dimensions.'

Forewarned of events, the observers on this occasion were singularly well-prepared to describe the scene for posterity.

Rather earlier, a particularly intrepid voyager on the high seas had a different kind of problem with a volcano about 1400 years ago. Among the many early voyagers who may or may not have been first to cross the Atlantic the Irish Saint Brendan was surely one of the most courageous. His voyages were made in the sixth century in leather boats, and it is most likely that he and his companions got at least as far as Iceland, the volcanic island of the north, as this description, which has been translated from a medieval Latin text, indicates: 'They came within view of an island, which was very rugged and rocky, covered over with slag, without trees or herbage, but full of smiths' forges . . . they heard the noise of bellows blowing like thunder . . . St Brendan said to his brethren, "Put on more sail,

Prudent Chinese families set up street shelters (below) and turned drainpipes into temporary – but earthquake-proof – houses (right).

and ply your oars more briskly, that we may get away from this island" . . . when they had passed on about a mile . . . the whole island seemed one globe of fire, and the sea on every side boiled up and foamed like a cauldron set on a fire well supplied with fuel.'

Small wonder that St Brendan's party thought themselves to be on the edge of Hell; today, one can appreciate that those sounds like a smithy were the work of neither man nor Devil, but of the forces of nature. There are few better images of this shaking Earth than St Brendan's 'cauldron set on a fire well supplied with fuel.' For that is exactly the situation. People live on a thin crust over a hot and active Earth, which is not solid at all but bubbling and heaving in the depths below, to produce, almost incidentally, the drama of volcanoes and earthquakes here above.

The New Madrid quake which hit near New Orleans in 1811, is also well documented in a graphic letter from a pioneer, Eliza Bryan: 'The Mississippi first seemed to recede from its banks, and its waters gathered up like a mountain, leaving for a moment many boats, which were on their way to New Orleans, on the bare sand, in which time the poor sailors made their escape from them.

Then, rising 15 or 20 feet perpendicularly and expanding, as it were, at the same time, the banks overflowed with a retrograde current rapid as a torrent. The boats, which before had been left on the sand, were now torn from their moorings . . . the river . . . took with it whole groves of young cottonwood trees . . . broken off with such regularity in some instances that persons who had not witnessed the fact could with difficulty be persuaded that it had not been the work of man. The river was literally covered with the wrecks of boats.'

Among its other effects, this quake created a new lake some 14 miles (22 kilometers) long and 4.5 miles (seven kilometers) wide, in a region that is today highly populated. A recurrence of such activity in the same site today would be far worse than the all-time classic earthquake, the 1906 disaster which hit San Francisco – and where quakes struck in the last century they can strike today.

After the greatest modern eruption – Krakatoa in 1883 – a French ship sails through a sea of bodies.

Not all eruptions, however, are destructive to man. In 1912 one of the greatest volcanic outbreaks of this century and, for that matter, of all recorded time, took place when Alaska's Katmai complex, part of the so-called 'ring of fire' which all but completely girdles the Pacific Ocean, blew its top. This eruption is one of the least known internationally and deserves some attention.

On 2 June the first earthquake shocks were felt in the village of Katmai. At first there was little cause for alarm, for in active volcanic areas such as the Aleutians and Alaska, earthquakes are not at all uncommon. People had learned to take them for granted. However, the interval between shocks shortened and the intensity increased to a point where they were considered severe on 4 and 5 June.

On the morning of 6 June the steamer *Dora* was making her way through the Shelikof Straits, bound for a stop at Kodiak. Captain C B McCullen made the following notes in the ship's log: 'At 1 o'clock pm while entering Kupreanot Straits, sighted a heavy cloud of smoke directly astern, raising from the Alaska Peninsula. . . . The smoke arose and spread in the sky following the vessel, and by 3.00 pm was directly over us. . . . At 6.30 pm ashes commenced to fall and in a few minutes we were in complete darkness not even the water over the ship's side could be seen. . . . Heavy thunder and lightning commenced early in the afternoon and continued throughout the night. Birds of all species kept falling on the deck in a helpless condition. The temperature rose owing to the heat of the volcanic ash, the latter penetrating into all parts of the ship, even down into the engine room.'

One of the few pictures ever taken during an earthquake. Shot on 5 August 1949, it shows the tower of the Cathedral in Ambato, Equador, crumbling.

THE EARTHQUAKES OF ENGLAND

No area on earth is utterly immune from earthquakes. They may be small and they may be rare, but they are there nevertheless, either as small shocks in their own right or as echoes of larger earthquakes elsewhere.

Britain, some of whose rocks are among the oldest on earth, is usually considered as one of the most stable areas in the world, yet it experiences several noticeable tremors every year. In 1912 there were over 70.

In 1884 Colchester was struck by an earthquake which was the most destructive shock that the country has ever experienced. It was felt over an area of a hundred thousand square miles and about 400 buildings were destroyed in Colchester alone. In surrounding villages, chimney stacks tumbled by the hundred.

No one, apparently, died as a result of the quake, and by comparison with the fully-fledged shakes described elsewhere in this book, it was an insignificant event; yet to those who lived through it, its very unfamiliarity made it horrific, as the following account taken from *The Essex Telegraph* of 26 April 1884, recalls:

'Colchester was thrown into a state of indescribable panic and alarm on Tuesday morning, April 22, by a shock of earthquake. The event occurred at twenty minutes past nine o'clock, and lasted several seconds. The ground was convulsed from one end of the town to the other, houses were shaken to their foundations, bells were set a-ringing, pictures dislodged from the walls, vases and ornaments on tables and cheffoniers overturned and thrown down, and hundreds of chimneys wrecked. It is impossible to exaggerate the feeling of consternation which prevailed. Everybody rushed into the open air, expecting to see visible results of the subterranean commotion and to be able instantaneously to divine the cause. Women shrieked in their terror and alarm in the most piercing manner, and strong men were utterly unnerved and paralysed . . . Master Herbert Johnson, son of Mr. Johnson, plumber, &c., Lion Walk, was standing at his door looking at the structure when the shock came. He saw the spire rent asunder, witnessed the air filled with the descending masonry, yet was so terrified that he was riveted to the spot, and at least one of the large blocks of stone fell at his very feet. . . . In the various schools of the town the scholars has only just assembled, and the shock was so terrible in the alarm and panic it produced among them that they were at once permitted to go to their respective homes, and the schools were closed for the day . . .

The sensations experienced by people in different parts of the town and neighbourhood appear to have been very varied and peculiar. In Mr. George Beaumont's timber yard in the Rawstorn Road the prostrate trees upon which workmen were engaged rolled from side to side . . . Mr. T. Street was making some drain communication in connection with certain cottages in Factory Lane, and while standing in the excavation he distinctly felt the subterraneous vibrations, while a drain-pipe which rested partly in his hand and partly on the earth flew completely over. Persons driving or riding out of doors were in some cases unaware that anything had happened until their ears were assailed with the shrieks of terrified women and children, who involuntarily rushed into the open air for safety. On the other hand persons walking along the pavements were nearly thrown down, the streets rose and fell with a wave-like motion, and substantial buildings rocked visibly.'

A ruined cottage at Abberton, a village four miles south of Colchester.

The account of Captain K W Perry, from the log of the US Coast Guard cutter *Manning*, continues the story. Captain Perry's entry of 7 June, when he was at Kodiak almost one hundred miles from the eruption center, states: 'All streams and wells have become choked, about five inches of ash having fallen, and water was furnished inhabitants by the *Manning* and by a schooner.

'At noon ashes began to fall again, increased until 1.00 pm. Visibility was 50 feet (15 meters). Abject terror took possession of the place. At 2.00 pm pitch darkness shut in. There was heavy static disturbances to the radio. No light appeared at dawn 8 June. Ash had been removed from the ship 7 June, but now decks, masts, yards, and lifeboats were loaded with flakes of fine dust of a yellowish color. Sulphurous fumes came at times in the air. Avalanches of ashes could be heard sliding on the neighboring hills sending forth clouds of suffocating dust. The crew kept at work with shovels, and four streams of water were kept playing incessantly to try to rid the ship of the ash. The dust fall was so heavy that a lantern could not be seen at arm's length.'

Things on land were no better. Ivan Orloff, an Aleutian native, was working at a fishing camp at Kaflia Bay, 35 miles (55 kilometers) from the eruption. The following are excerpts from a letter to his wife on 9 June.

'We are waiting death at any moment. A mountain has burst near here. We are covered in ashes, in some place 10 feet and 6 feet (3–2 meters) deep. All this began 6 June. Night and day we light lanterns. We cannot see the daylight. We have no water, the rivers are just ashes mixed with water. Here are darkness and hell, thunder and noise. I do not know whether it is day or night. The earth is trembling, it lightens every minute. It is terrible. We are praying.'

Many varieties of animals, both wild and domestic, were blinded by the acid-forming vapors in the air and starved to death. Bears, crazed with hunger, attacked cattle. Salmon died in rivers and creeks, and birds fell dead out of the air.

Near the eruptions, the force of the initial blasts leveled trees like tenpins. All that was left was a gray monotone of drifting ash, a landscape of lunar desolation.

Just what was occurring in the wilderness? The increasingly violent earthquake shocks of 2, 3, and 4 June indicated that large-scale crustal shifts were occurring to accommodate tremendous gas and magma pressures, which reached the point where escape had become inevitable.

The face of one of the mountains, Falling Mountain, suddenly dropped. From the head of a wooded green valley, which was shortly to have thousands of smoking fumaroles (after which the place is now renamed the Valley of Ten Thousand Smokes), a tremendous avalanche of rock fragments swept down, leveling everything before it.

Then a vent, later named Novarupta, opened at the southeast end of the valley, violently spewing forth rhyolitic ash and pumice as an incandescent rock froth. Huge quantities of volatile material vaporized, and at one o'clock on 6 June 1912, the first of three culminating explosions shook the earth and the air. Novarupta's first big blast was heard at Ketchikan, 900 miles (1500 kilometers) to the east and at Dawson, some 650 miles (1000 kilometers) to the north. It has been estimated that within a period of a short 60 hours nearly seven cubic miles (45 cubic kilometers) of rock had been ejected from Novarupta and the fissures in the valley floor were covered with depths of up to 700 feet (215 meters) of ejecta.

So the catalog of catastrophe grows: explosions that deafen, waves in the 'solid' ground that throw a person off his feet, rivers that change course and new lakes that suddenly appear, fires that rage like Hell itself, and the man-made extras of further conflagration, panic and looting. The natural reaction – the logical approach – would surely be to keep well away from the regions of the Earth where such events take place. But that is not the way of mankind. Faced with adversity, by and large, mankind shows a stubborn opposition to the forces of nature. Knock down San Francisco and it is rebuilt; raise the puzzle of why some parts of the globe suffer such devastation and not others, and mankind endeavors to find out why the Earth shakes in this way. The answers have been a long time coming, but at last they seem to be clear. The whys and wherefores of earthquakes and volcanoes are understood today better than ever before. The next step – regular prediction to minimize the disastrous effects of such upheavals – is just around the corner. And the whole picture depends upon the fact that the Earth is not solid at all – that the very continents themselves drift about on the surface of a molten globe, carried hither and thither by the slow stirring of currents in the fluid beneath.

Survivors after an earthquake that killed 8000 people near Lake Van, Turkey, in November 1976.

VICTIMS OF DISASTER

This documentary portfolio was compiled to focus on the plight of the individual in the face of catastrophe. As pictures of shattered buildings and twisted roadways can never do, these pictures dramatize the emotional impact of the loss of life, the loss of property, and the loss all too often of a complete world.

Two victims – father and child – await burial.

Far left: Distraught, a ruined householder appeals to the heavens after the 1976 earthquake that shattered Gemona, northern Italy.

Left: While troops search for survivors after the Skopje, Yugoslavia, earthquake of July 1963, a family sits amidst their salvaged possessions.

Below: Three blocks of masonry jut up from a partially crushed car after an earthquake in Tuscania, 50 miles northwest of Rome, in February 1971

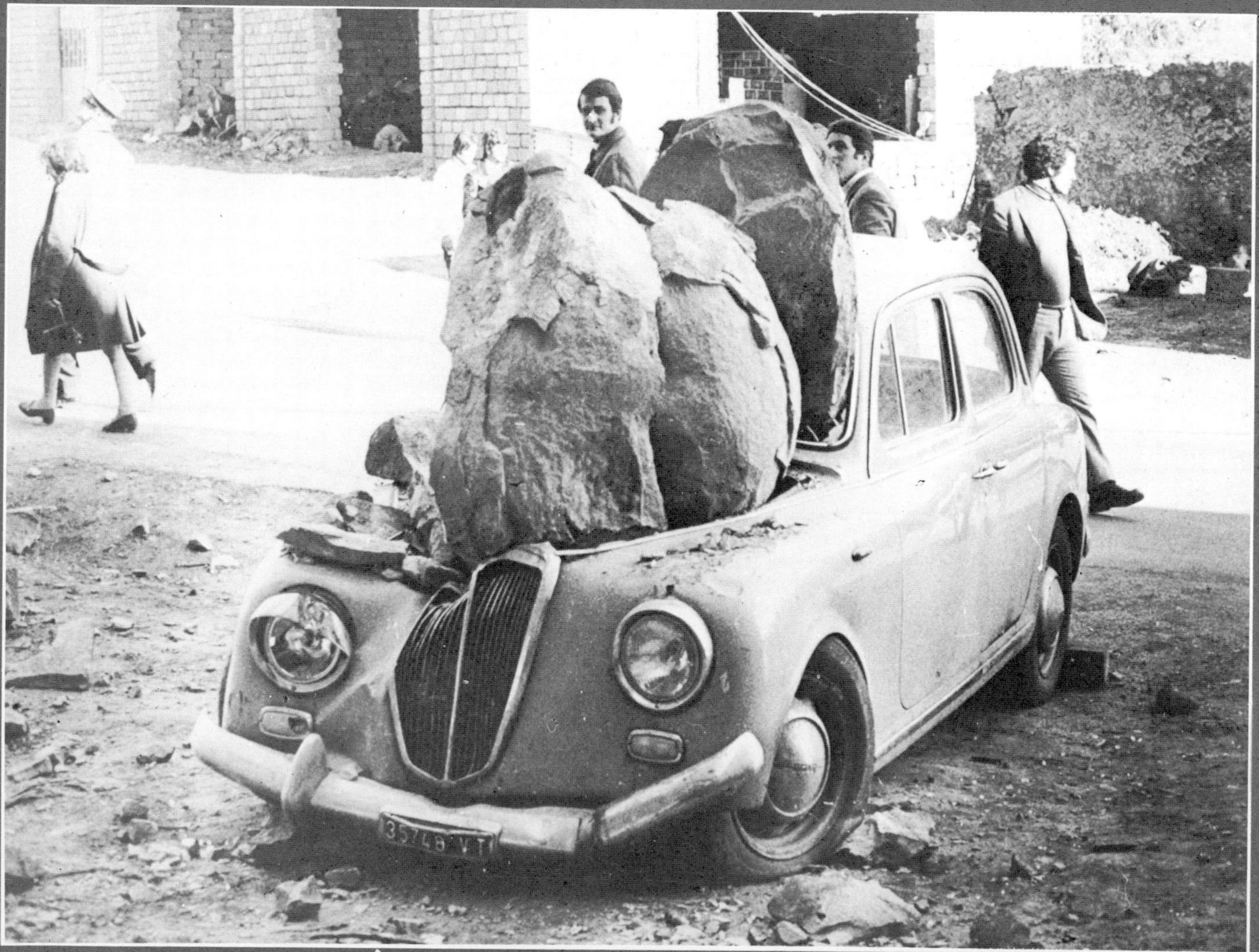

After the earthquake in Guatemala City in March 1976, a family gathers in front of a former home.

Turkey, 1966: Survivors discover the buried corpse of a little girl.

On the outskirts of Guatemala City, a mother filters drinking water for her family from a broken main.

During an eruption of Etna in March 1947, the inhabitants of a village at the foot of the mountain pray as lava rolls slowly towards their homes. On

this occasion, the eruption was brief and their homes were saved.

A satellite shot of the Indian sub-continent – the visible part of a continental plate that has been torn away from Africa and rammed into Asia (top), creating the Himalayas.

2: CRUST AND CRUMBLE

During the past few years, extraordinary discoveries in the earth sciences have transformed our understanding of our planet. This chapter explains and explores the revolutionary theory of continental drift, the inexorable forces that produce earthquakes and volcanoes, and the benefits they can offer to industrialized societies.

To anyone much below the age of 35, with a reasonable scientific education, the idea of the land beneath our feet moving about the globe like stirred up pieces of a spherical jigsaw is so well rooted as to be 'commonsense.' But this commonsense picture of the nature of continental drift was arrived at only in the middle of the 1960s, even though it was mooted a hundred years earlier, and had been the subject of fierce controversy for 50 years, off and on, since the pioneering work of the German scientist Alfred Wegener. Why were the ideas which now seem obvious so controversial for so long – and why did the scientific establishment suddenly come to accept them about ten years ago? It seems that this is a classic example of an idea being ahead of its time. To look at the way in which the world was persuaded of the reality of continental drift is as good a way as any of explaining today's theories of the Earth's structure.

Legend has it that one of the first people to notice the similarity in shape of the South American and African coastlines, on either side of the south Atlantic Ocean was Francis Bacon in 1620 (although he does not seem to have suggested that the similarity is the result of the continents' splitting and moving apart). This jigsaw-puzzle-like fit has been a source of inspiration and speculation for continental drifters since the first more-or-less scientific theory of such a drift was outlined in 1858. It was formulated by an American, Antonio Snider, who tied his ideas in with the Biblical tale of the Great Flood.

Snider's theory envisaged a single great land mass before the Flood, slowly being hardened and split open by internal heat, producing great cracks edged by volcanoes. Eventually the land mass rifted apart and the region of Atlantis was shifted violently westward to form the Americas, while the waters of the Flood rushed into the crack between the old world and the new. Some of these ideas look silly today; others, notably the concept of the Earth splitting along lines of volcanic activity, fit securely into the modern picture of continental drift, under its new name of 'plate tectonics.'

But in spite of the interest of Snider and a handful of other nineteenth century scientists in continental drift, the idea never really got off the ground. Various theories involved the splitting off of the Moon from what is now the Pacific Ocean basin and/or the passage of another planet close by the Earth triggering huge tidal forces, to 'explain' the catastrophic rifting of the Atlantic common to these ideas. But only in the early twentieth century, when Wegener put forward a coherent, self-consistent picture of how continental drift may have occurred was the geological establishment threatened enough to respond fully, blasting Wegener with a fury usually reserved for those who strike at the roots of a religious faith, not proponents of new scientific theories.

Wegener's big 'mistake' – and the reason his ideas met such a hot reception – seems to have been that he was an outsider, an astronomer who had turned to meteorology as his main work. In the eyes of many established geologists he was an amateur who had no business thinking about the nature of the solid Earth.

This late 19th century diagram attempts to explain geological change. It duly notes the significance of volcanoes (10, 11) and earthquakes (12), which are associated with 'elevations of land', but there is no mention of an underlying mechanism that would explain both phenomena. One item – rocks being transported by waves (7) – now seems pure fantasy

1. Evaporation, forming rain.
2. Decomposition of rocks by rain.
3. Removal of rocks by water.

4. Rivers.
5. Formation of deltas.
6. Destruction of coast by sea.
7. Drifting of large masses of rocks under influence of waves.
8. Formation of sandhills by the tides.
9. Landslips.
10. Volcanoes.
11. Submarine volcanoes.
12. Earthquakes and elevations of land.
13. Formations of coral reefs.
14. Glaciers.
15. Icebergs.
16. Transport of solid material by river ice.

Fortunately the difficulties do not seem to be quite so great today, for as it happens, the evidence for continental drift can *only* be seen in its full glory by someone with interdisciplinary interests. In that sense, the delay in acceptance of the theory may have been a result of overspecialization.

So what is this variety of evidence? At Wegener's time – his ideas were published in 1912 and developed further over the next two decades – there was already much more to the story than the simple jigsaw-puzzle fit of the continents. When the pieces of the puzzle are fitted together in the way they are imagined to have been joined millions or even hundreds of millions of years ago, the land on either side of the join matches up in quite remarkable detail, especially in the case of South America and Africa, which has come to provide the classic example. The standard analogy is to imagine a jigsaw puzzle, with pieces shaped like the modern continents made from torn-up pieces of newspaper. Just fitting the pieces together does not necessarily prove that they 'belong' together; but when it is found that by fitting the pieces corresponding to South America and Africa together in a certain way, the lines of print in the newspaper story join up from one 'continent' to the other without a break, then surely the evidence is overwhelming. To those today, maybe, but not, it seems, to the opponents of Wegener in the years from 1912 to the 1960s. Yet the number of 'lines' that joined up to tell a coherent 'story' should have provided an overwhelming weight of evidence.

First, the kinds of rock themselves continue from one continent across the join and into the other. With the appropriate fit, old rocks in South America lie next to old rocks in Africa, and young rocks next to young rocks. Second, the evidence of a great former period of glaciation can be found in the rocks not only of South America and Africa but also Australia, Antarctica and India. The rock strata laid down during this ice age, between about 200 and 350 million years ago, can be clearly distinguished in all of these continents, and the area they cover can be accounted for very nicely by a region of glaciation around the South Pole – but only if those continents were stuck together, and roughly centered over the pole, at the critical period 200–350 million years ago. More evidence comes from the remains of living organisms found on different continents; coal beds and fossil remains also match up across the 'join,' including remains of identical creatures that lived only in freshwater, now separated by the salty expanse of the Atlantic Ocean.

With evidence like this, its hard to see how the theory of continental drift could fail to be taken seriously. But there was an alternative, which was just barely plausible enough to provide a standby for those geologists hidebound by tradition, at least for as long as the ocean floors remained a mysterious and largely unknown feature of the surface of our planet Earth.

This desperate alternative to continental drift is the concept of 'land bridges' and it really does look desperate with hindsight and the benefit of modern knowledge about the sea bed. In this picture, the similarities between the rocks and past inhabitants of two continents now separated by ocean were ex-

Far right: A satellite shot of the Persian Gulf – an area in which the crust of the earth is literally being torn apart by subterranean forces.

plained in terms of the sinking below the sea of a solid land bridge that used to join the continents. Somehow the central region of land must have sunk below the ocean waves, breaking the connection between the two distant land masses. According to this theory, the ocean floor should have the same kind of crust on its surface as solid land, but be covered with water. *Vertical* movements of the crust were quite acceptable to the geological orthodoxy 60 years ago, but the idea of *horizontal* movements was heretical. The reason for these movements was thought to be that the Earth, formed in a molten state, was still cooling and contracting, with mountain chains forming like the wrinkles on the skin of a drying apple, and the great collapse of the regions now seen as ocean basins caused by the squeeze of the surrounding, contracting crust on weak parts of the skin.

Wegener's theory, on the other hand, envisaged the continents plowing through the weaker crust of the ocean floor like icebergs plowing through the sea. For this theory two completely different kinds of crust around the molten interior of planet Earth are required: the thick crust of the continents and a much thinner skin forming the ocean floor. It is not easy to accept the idea of 'solid' ocean floor crust flowing to allow the passage of the continents, but there are many substances which show the kind of behavior that would be necessary. One obvious example is the silicon based 'magic' putty that was popular a few years ago – a rubbery substance that bounced if rolled into a ball or thrown against a wall, flowed slowly downhill if left in one place, and would shatter like glass if struck sharply with a hammer. The relevant lesson is that the behavior of 'solid' rocks on human time-scales may be quite different from their behavior when subjected to steady pressure over millions of years.

So here was a clear way to distinguish between the rival theories. Wegener's statistical studies showed quite conclusively that there are indeed two kinds of Earth crust: one lying at an average elevation typical of the continents, and the other lying at a quite different average, appropriate to the crust of the ocean floors. This alone is sufficient to disprove the idea that land bridges, identical to the surrounding continents, sank below the oceans while mountains were raised elsewhere by uplift; if that were the case, there would be only one average elevation, with all the crust distributed evenly around the average. The crucial evidence was there, even in the 1920s.

But the inertia of the established view prevailed for a further 40 years while more and more evidence accumulated. It turned out, in the end, that Wegener's idea of continents moving through the ocean crust is not quite correct, and it is the crucial difference between that idea and the modern one that gives the modern theory the name 'plate tectonics' and allows former opponents of Wegener's ideas to embrace the new version without too much loss of face. But once again the key to the establishment of the modern theory comes from the study of the ocean floor.

Insight into the modern theory of plate tectonics both explains why volcanoes and earthquakes occur where they do and offers hope of predicting the occurrence of these often disastrous quivers of the shaking Earth. Two pieces of evidence seem to have combined, in the early 1960s, to make the idea of continental drift acceptable. First, Sir Edward Bullard and his colleagues at the University of Cambridge produced a 'new' fit of the continents on either side of the Atlantic – a reconstruction of the prehistoric jigsaw puzzle rather like Wegener's, but this time made with the aid of a modern electronic computer.

A 17th-century drawing correctly associates earthquakes with a tidal wave, but falsely links both to a fire-and-brimstone climatic catastrophe. This view derives from Aristotle's belief that earthquakes were caused by winds bottled up in the bowels of the earth.

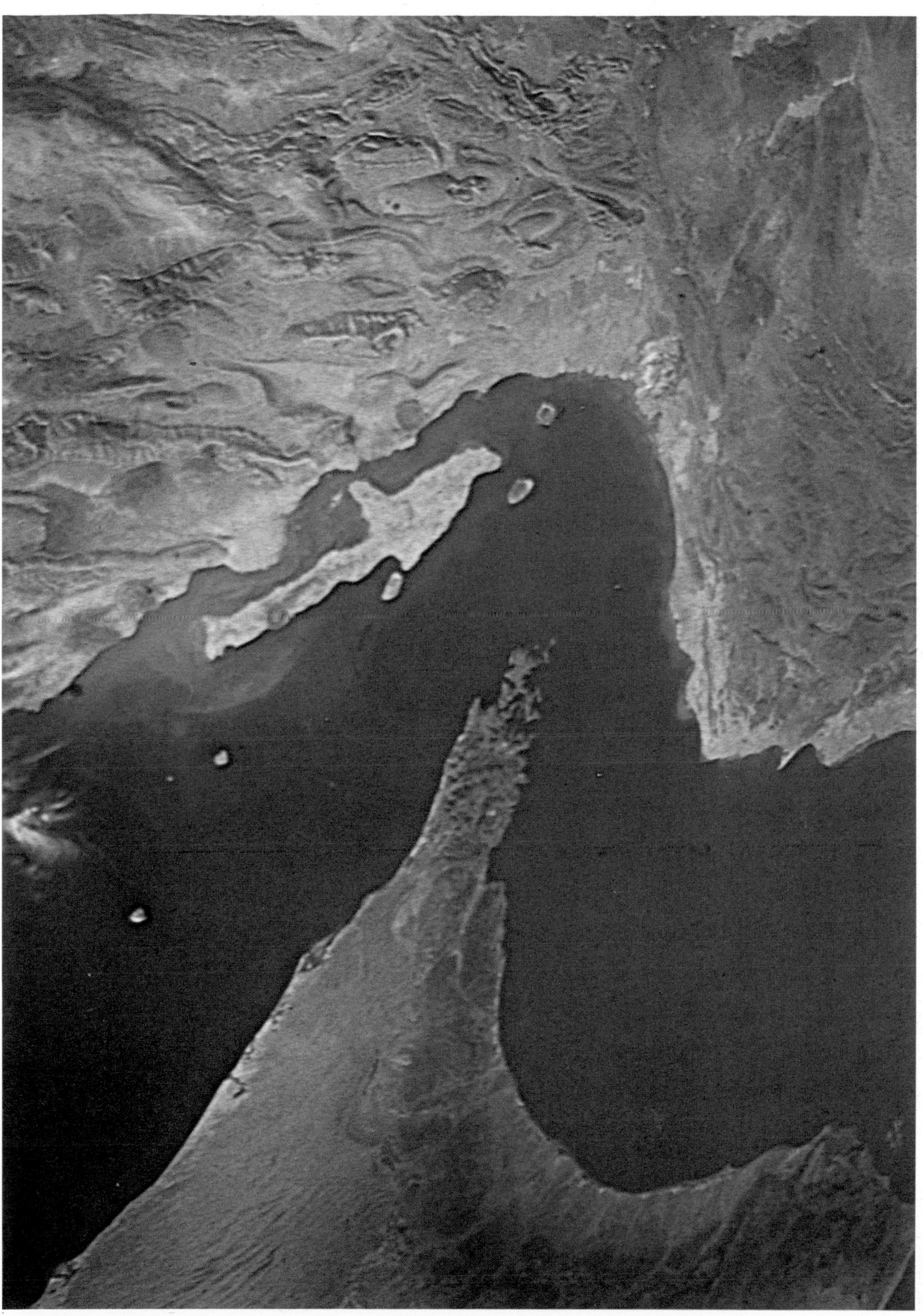

WEGENER'S DRIFTING CONTINENTS

The credit for establishing the theory of continental drift must go to Alfred Wegener, a German geologist, meteorologist, balloonist and polar explorer. His wide experience and interests led him to make generalizations that struck his over-specialized critics as mere fantasy. His theories were largely dismissed as merely eccentric by the time of his death on the Greenland icecap in 1930. His details were, not surprisingly, faulty – he did not for instance, see India as a separate 'block.' Yet in general his theory, put forward in successive editions of his *Origin of Continents and Oceans*, seems now remarkably modern.

'Where does the truth lie? The earth at any one time can only have had one configuration. Were there land bridges then or were the continents separated by broad stretches of ocean, as today? It is impossible to deny the postulate of former land bridges if we do not want to abandon wholly the attempt to understand the evolution of life on earth. But it is also impossible to overlook the grounds on which the exponents of permanence deny the existence of sunken intermediate continents. There clearly remains but one possibility: there must be a hidden error in the assumptions alleged to be obvious.

'This is the starting point of displacement or drift theory. The basic "obvious" supposition common to both land-bridge and permanence theory – that the relative position of the continents, disregarding their variable shallow-water cover, has never altered – must be wrong. The continents must have shifted. South America must have lain alongside a cracked ice floe in water. The edges of these two blocks are even today strikingly congruent. Not only does the large rectangular bend formed by the Brazilian coast at Cape São Roque mate exactly with the bend in the African coast at the Cameroons, but also south of these two corresponding points every projection on the Brazilian side matches a congruent bay on the African, and conversely. . . .

'In the same way, North America at one time lay alongside Europe and formed a coherent block with it and Greenland, at least from Newfoundland and Ireland northwards. . . . Antarctica, Australia and India up to the beginning of the Jurassic lay alongside southern Africa and formed together with it and South America a single large continent, partly covered by shallow water. This block split off into separate blocks in the course of the Jurassic, Cretaceous and Tertiary, and the sub-blocks drifted away in all directions. . . . In the case of India the process was somewhat different: originally it was joined to Asia by a long stretch of land, mostly under shallow water. After the separation of India from Australia on the one hand (in the early Jurassic) and from Madagascar on the other (at the transition from Tertiary to Cretaceous), this long junction zone became increasingly folded by the continuing approach of present-day India to Asia; it is now the largest folded range on earth, i.e., the Himalaya and the many other folded chains of upland Asia.

'There are also other areas where the continental drift is linked causally with orogenesis. In the westward drift of both Americas, their leading edges were compressed and folded by the frontal resistance of the ancient Africa and formed a unified block which was split in two in the Cretaceous; the two parts must then have become increasingly separated over a period of millions of years like pieces of

Alfred Wegener (right) and a motorized sled used on his expeditions to Greenland (below).

Today, it seems rather odd that the mere use of a computer should have added such weight to the argument, but several special factors have to be born in mind.

Not least of these is that opponents of the concept had always argued that the theory rested upon circumstantial evidence, and, worse, a *subjective* interpretation of the evidence. Use of a computer seemed to rule out the subjective element (although, since the machine is programed by humans, it is no more true to say that an electronic computer is always 'objective' than it is to say that the camera 'cannot lie'!). The actual 'fit' of the continents was made not at the present day shorelines, which vary as the sea-level changes, but at the edge of the continental shelf, where the boundary between the two kinds of Earth's crusts lies, and there is no denying that it is a good fit. But in addition to this supposed 'objectivity,' it may be that Bullard's reconstruction was seen, perhaps subconsciously, as an excuse to be persuaded. The jigsaw puzzle evidence was really no better than it had been for 50 years; but a weight of other evidence must have been preparing the minds of all but the most stubborn non-drifters for a change. Bullard's

Pacific floor, which was deeply chilled and hence a source of viscous drag. The result was the vast Andean range which extends from Alaska to Antarctica. Consider also the case of the Australian block, including New Guinea, which is separated only by a shelf sea: on the leading side, relative to the direction of displacement, one finds the high-altitude New Guinea range, a recent formation. Before this block split away from Antarctica, its direction was a different one. The present-day east coastline was then the leading side. At that time New Zealand, which was directly in front of this coast, had its mountains formed by folding. Later as a result of the change in direction of displacement, the mountains were cut off and left behind as island chains. . . . smaller portions of blocks are left behind during continental drift, particularly when it is in a westerly direction. For instance, the marginal chains of East Asia split off as island arcs, the Lesser and Greater Antilles were left behind by the drift of the Central American block, and so was the so-called Southern Antilles arc (South Shetlands) between Tierra del Fuego and western Antarctica. In fact, all blocks which taper off towards the south exhibit a bend in the taper in an easterly direction because the tip has trailed behind. examples are the southern tip of Greenland, the Florida shelf, Tierra del Fuego, the Graham coast [of Antarctica] and the continental fragment of Ceylon.

'It is easy to see that the whole idea of drift theory starts out from the supposition that deep-sea floors and continents consist of different materials and are, as it were, different layers of the earth's structure. The outermost layer, represented by the continental blocks, does not cover the whole earth's surface, or it may be truer to say that it no longer does so. The ocean floors represent the free surface of the next layer inwards, which is also assumed to run under the blocks. This is the geophysical aspect of drift theory.'

suggestion removed the last brick from opinions already prepared to tumble.

The key reason for this prepared state of mind was the second crucial piece of evidence, which concerned the magnetism of the sea floor. Studies of magnetized rocks – paleomagnetic studies – had already shown that such old rocks have, in many cases, moved relative to the Earth's magnetic field since they were laid down. It is simple now to understand the process by which these rocks provide a kind of 'fossil magnetism' marking the orientation of the field millions of years ago. Molten rock, welling up from the Earth's hot interior and spreading out through volcanic vents, may contain iron minerals or other magnetizable materials. As the molten rock – magma – sets it will take on a weak magnetism, aligned by the Earth's magnetic field. But, once it is set, this magnetism remains fixed. By studying old rocks – whose age is known from other means – it is possible to map out the orientation of the rocks relative to the poles when it was laid down. Although the magnetic poles do wander slightly, they never move very far from the geographic poles – yet in many cases paleomagnetic studies reveal a magnetic

It is now generally accepted that the continents have been drifting since they were formed, perhaps 4000 million years ago. Little, however, is certain before about 500 million years ago, and a common baseline of geological history has become the break-up of the super-continent Pangaea, some 200 million years ago. The collisions between the continental plates that formed Pangaea created mountain ranges of once towering peaks, now scrubbed almost flat by erosion, like the Appalachians and the Urals. Later collisions between continental plates formed recent mountain ranges like the Rockies, the Andes, the Alps and the Himalayas. The outlines of the continents before the formation of Pangaea are not known and are here given their present-day shapes.

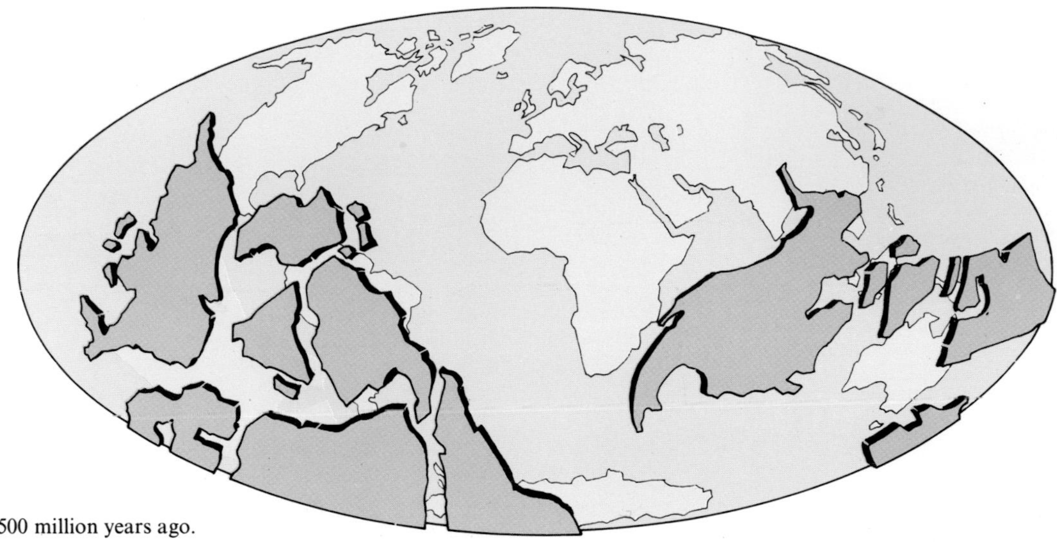

500 million years ago.

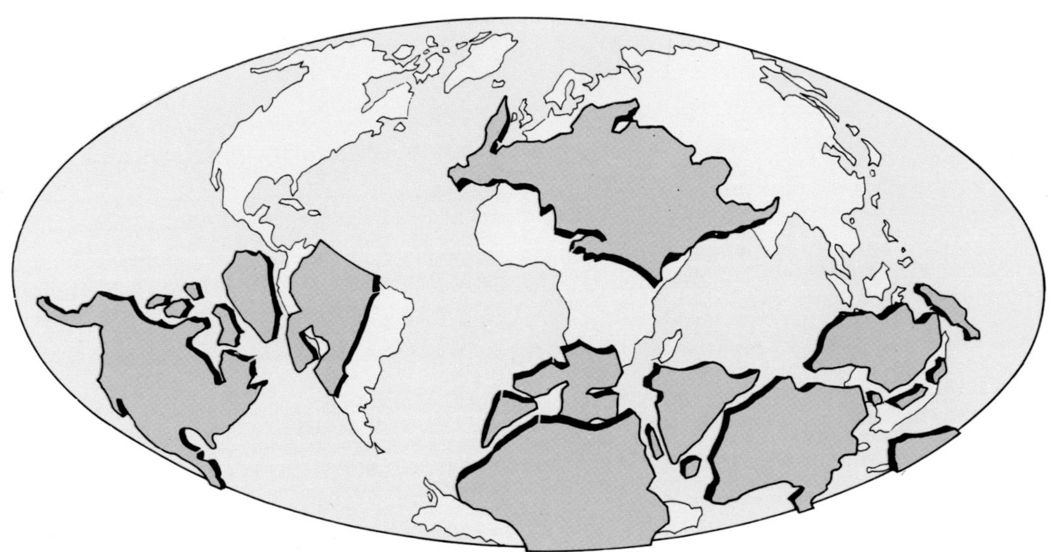

400 million years ago.

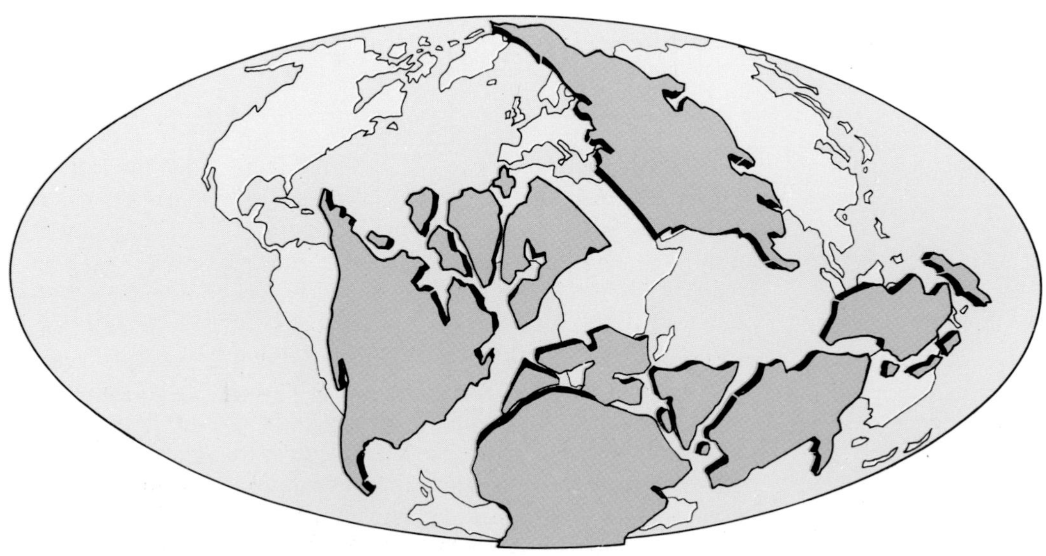

300 million years ago.

500 million years ago
The continents are scattered across the face of the earth.

400 million years ago
Continental islands swing around prior to collision.

300 million years ago
The formation of the super-continent of Pangaea ('All land').

200 million years ago
Pangaea begins to break into sections recognizable as today's continental masses.

140 million years ago
South America begins to separate from Africa to form a primitive South Atlantic.

65 million years ago
South America is well clear of Africa but Australia and Antarctica are still joined, as are North America and Europe.

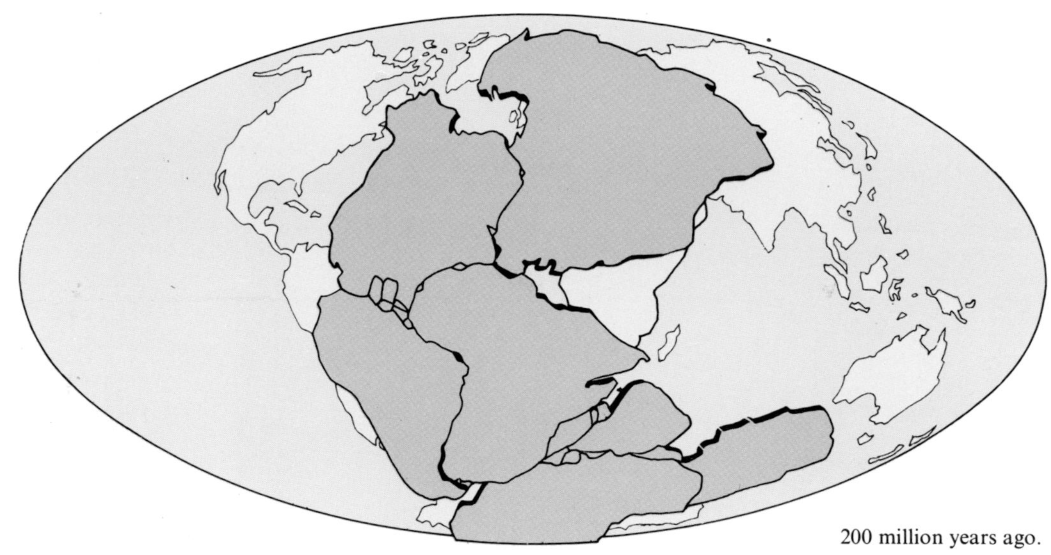

200 million years ago.

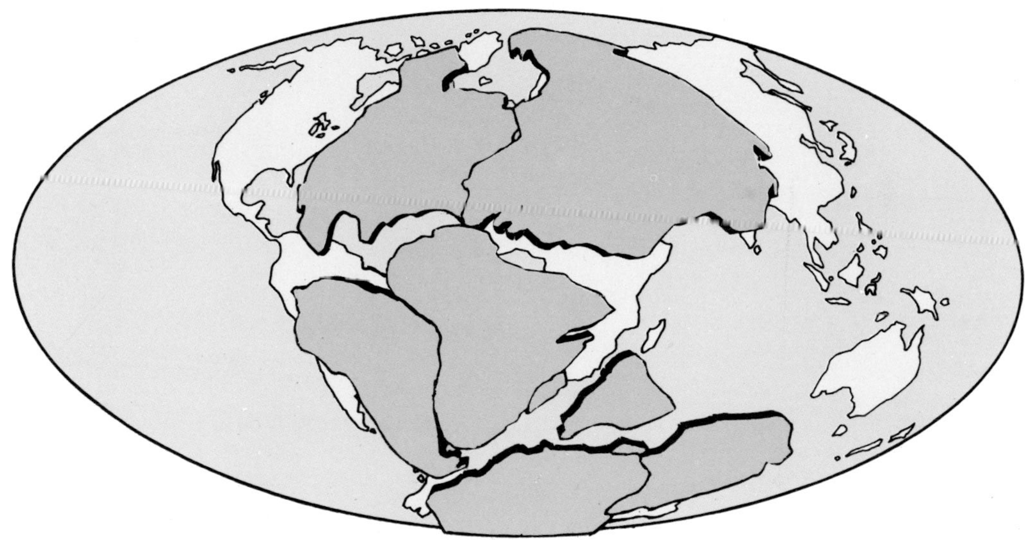

140 million years ago.

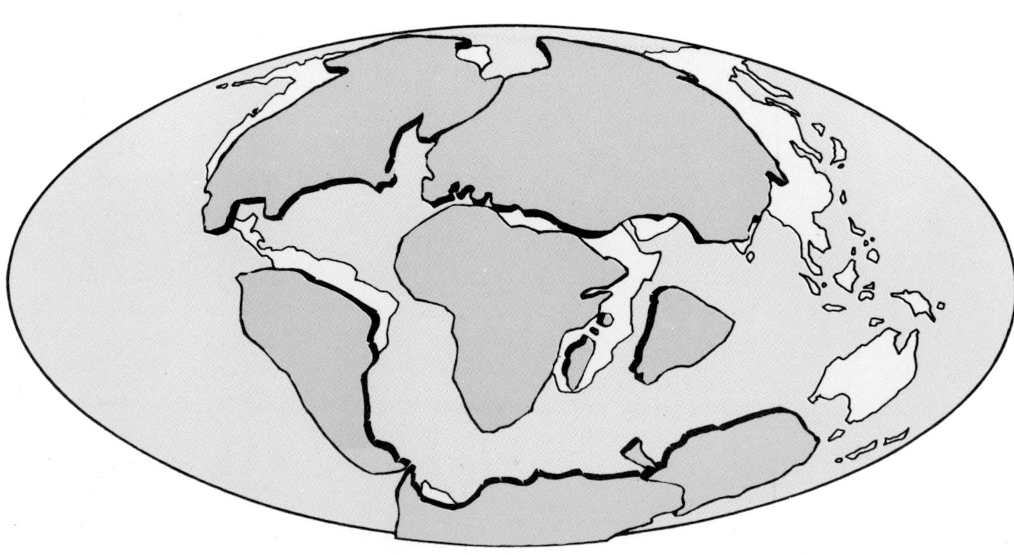

65 million years ago.

The Giant's Causeway in County Antrim, Northern Ireland: an example of basalt, a fine-grained rock, which magnetizes strongly when it emerges molten from within the earth at the mid-oceanic ridges. Basalt's magnetic 'stripes', which build up as the rock is pushed outwards from the ridges, provided prime evidence for continental drift in the 1960s.

orientation in old rocks completely different from the orientation of the Earth's magnetic field today. If the magnetic poles have not moved vast distances, the only alternative is that the solid rocks have been shifted about the face of the Earth since they set – powerful evidence in favor of horizontal movements and continental drift. Lining up magnetic rocks across the joins in the jigsaw puzzle provides one way to read the 'newspaper' when the puzzle is reconstructed. But when new techniques opened up the possibility of studying the magnetism of the ocean floors, the evidence gained finally became overwhelmingly convincing, and at the same time hinted at the underlying mechanism driving the drift.

The types of rock that provide the most significant evidence are basaltic rocks. Basalts are weakly magnetic rocks, and the ocean floor is largely composed of basalts. (Incidentally, further evidence of the two kinds of crust continued to mount with the discovery that these basalts form a thin but dense crust quite unlike the thicker, lighter continental crust; but for some reason that piece of evidence did not catch the geologists' imagination sufficiently to convince the skeptics on its own.) Although the practical difficulties are by no means insignificant, it has proved possible in the past couple of decades to measure the direction of the magnetism in the rocks from many parts of the ocean floor, and a dramatic picture emerges.

On land, where successive layers of rock have been piled one on top of another by volcanism and other geological activity, the paleomagnetic studies show, in many cases, that successive layers of rock have exactly the opposite direction of magnetization. The top layer, naturally enough, is oriented in line with the present north and south magnetic poles; but a deeper layer may have opposite polarity, aligned with a magnetic field in which north and south poles were reversed; still deeper, there are layers again in line with the present magnetic field; and so the pattern goes on.

The cause of this pattern is clear, even though the physics behind it remains slightly mysterious. From time to time, the magnetic field of the Earth dies away to nothing, then builds up again in the opposite direction so that the 'north' magnetic pole may be in the southern hemisphere, with the 'south' magnetic pole in the north. Whatever the physics of the mechanism, the process gives geologists a means to date rock layers precisely. Once the layers in one sample of rock strata from a well-studied continental site are dated, they can be calibrated against the magnetic reversals. Then, by counting the magnetic reversals in the same way tree rings are counted to find the age of a tree, the age of rocks in strata from other sites can also be found.

When paleomagnetists applied this technique to the basalts of the ocean floor, however, they made a remarkable discovery. Instead of successively older strata lying one on top of the other like the continental rocks, the basalts of the sea floor tend to be spread out on either side of large oceanic ridges – with older basalts furthest from the ridge, and new, young rocks next to the ridge itself. The magnetic 'tape recorder' shows convincingly that rocks are laid down on these active ridges – where geologists already knew great volcanic and earthquake activity was occurring – and are then pushed off to either side, making way for still younger rocks to push in behind. New crust is, literally, created at the ocean ridges and spreads out pushing the oceans wider apart, and shoving the continents bodily along for the ride.

This concept of the spreading sea floor came as a bombshell to geology and geophysics in the early 1960s, and indicates, more than anything else, the difference between the modern theory of plate tectonics and the old idea of continental drift with the continents drifting *through* the sea-floor basalts like icebergs through the sea.

But one big question is raised by the new discovery – what happens to all the new ocean floor basalt continuously being created? Is the Earth expanding to accommodate ever more crust? Or is crust destroyed somewhere else so that there is a constant balance of the two flows?

It now seems that the second alternative is the correct one. Just as new crust is created at the ocean ridges, so old sea floor is destroyed at the deep ocean trenches which mark the boundaries between some oceans and continents, notably the region near Japan. At these sites, sea floor, thrust inexorably outward from the ocean-spreading ridge, meets the immovable object of a continental mass and is pushed back down into the bowels of the Earth, breaking up and melting as it goes. The continents are now seen as largely indestructible and permanent, although they may grow slightly through the ages as mountains are pushed up by this activity at deep trenches. Continually pushed apart then thrust back into new patterns by the restless surging of the ocean floor basalts, the continents remain composed of largely the same old rocks, while the sea floors are constantly destroyed and renewed. All geological tests confirm this picture: around the world continental rocks are, by and large, old rocks, while sea-floor rocks are invariably young rocks.

So now the broad outline of the picture is complete. The continents on which we live are solid rafts, like crusts on a pan of porridge, being jostled about by the activity of the molten Earth below and the ocean crust on either side. When continents are pushed together, mountains may be upthrust in the collision; equally, where a continent meets a deep trench into which (relatively) old ocean crust is diving it may crumple up to form mountains, as has happened down the western coast of South America. Magma from the Earth's interior wells up at the ocean ridges and spreads on either side, solidifying as crust before diving back into an ocean trench, melting and completing the cycle. Local effects wherever mountains are built can release magma through volcanic activity, as discussed in Chapter 4, and these sites are typically near the deep ocean trenches. Here, then, is the answer to the puzzle that has plagued mankind for centuries – why do volcanoes and earthquakes occur where they do, in fairly narrow, well-defined belts? One now sees that these belts of geological activity mark the boundaries where new ocean crust is either being created or destroyed – the 'plate boundaries' in the new jargon. Down the ocean ridges (which sometimes break surface, as in the geologically active and literally expanding island of Iceland), around the deep trenches (Japan and the Far East, the west of South America and so on) and where two lumps are being squeezed together (notably the shrinking Mediterranean, and the Himalayas) are all places where earthquakes and volcanoes must inevitably occur. Equally, far from any active boundaries in the middle of one of the geological plates things should be pretty quiet – as, indeed, they are in England or (with the exception of some interesting special cases like Hawaii) the middle of the Pacific.

As far as *people* are concerned, the ocean ridges are of the least interest – a major earthquake in the middle of the Atlantic is only going to bother the fishes (although one must always remember the special case of Iceland – discussed in more detail in a later chapter – where there are people living on a piece of ocean ridge, and where the juxtaposition of volcanoes and sea water raises special problems). The most dramatic effects, in human terms, occur where continents collide. Most of the mountain ranges of the present continents are thought to be the results of earlier collisions between quite different continents in previous cycles of tectonic activity, and these mark the boundaries between the older continents, sites where seas have been squeezed out of existence. But, in many ways the most interesting regions of geological activity are those sites where two plates of the Earth's crust rub side by side, twisting and nudging against one another without any major creation or destruction of oceanic crust. Just such an active region is found on the west coast of America where the American plate rubs shoulders with the great Pacific plate; the 'dotted line' joining the two runs through the state of California in the form of the notorious San Andreas Fault, responsible for the great San Francisco disaster of 1906.

But the effects of the continental drift should not be seen solely in terms of disasters. Earthquakes and volcanoes – and the forces that produce them – are also great providers. The fruits of tectonic activity are harvested to feed industrialized society today.

POWERS THAT MOVE THE EARTH'S CRUST

The theory that, since 1965, has won almost universal acceptance as a general explanation for the major features of the earth's surface is known as plate tectonics – the construction of the earth's geological features by the action of plates. The plates are shown at right and the mechanisms that drive them in the cross-section below, which details a cut through the earth's crust from California to Hawaii to China. In brief, the theory is as follows:

The outermost 40 miles or so of the earth consists almost entirely of cool solid rock like the shell of a nut, which is divided into plates. Hot fluid rock from inside the earth keeps the plates jostling about against each other. Little change occurs in the middle of the plates. All the action is round the edges, where most of the earthquakes and volcanoes occur (in particular round the Pacific Plate, the so-called Ring of Fire). No gap can exist between the plates. If one drifts away from another, hot rock instantly rises to fill the gap. Nor do plates overlap much. If plates collide, one of them dips and its material re-enters the earth's interior at a steep angle at what is called an ocean trench. As it sinks, it causes earthquakes and volcanoes. There are three kinds of plate boundary: sea-floor ridges where two plates are manufactured at the same time; ocean trenches; and transform faults (i.e., the San Andreas Fault) in which two plates slide past one another.

The continents ride as passengers on the plates. Though the plates they travel on are destroyed, the continents themselves cannot sink because they are made of lighter rock. Continental rocks are therefore much older than the rocks of the ocean floor. When continents collide, they form mountain chains, which remain until eroded.

In this cross-sectional view of the Pacific plate, Hawaii represents a 'hot-spot' in the crust, where active volcanoes are formed continuously. These are then blocked and carried away by the newly formed sea-floor crust. On the right where the Pacific plate meets California there is no subduction zone: the two plates grind past each other without overriding. On the left, a meeting of three plates explains the geological volatility of Japan and China.

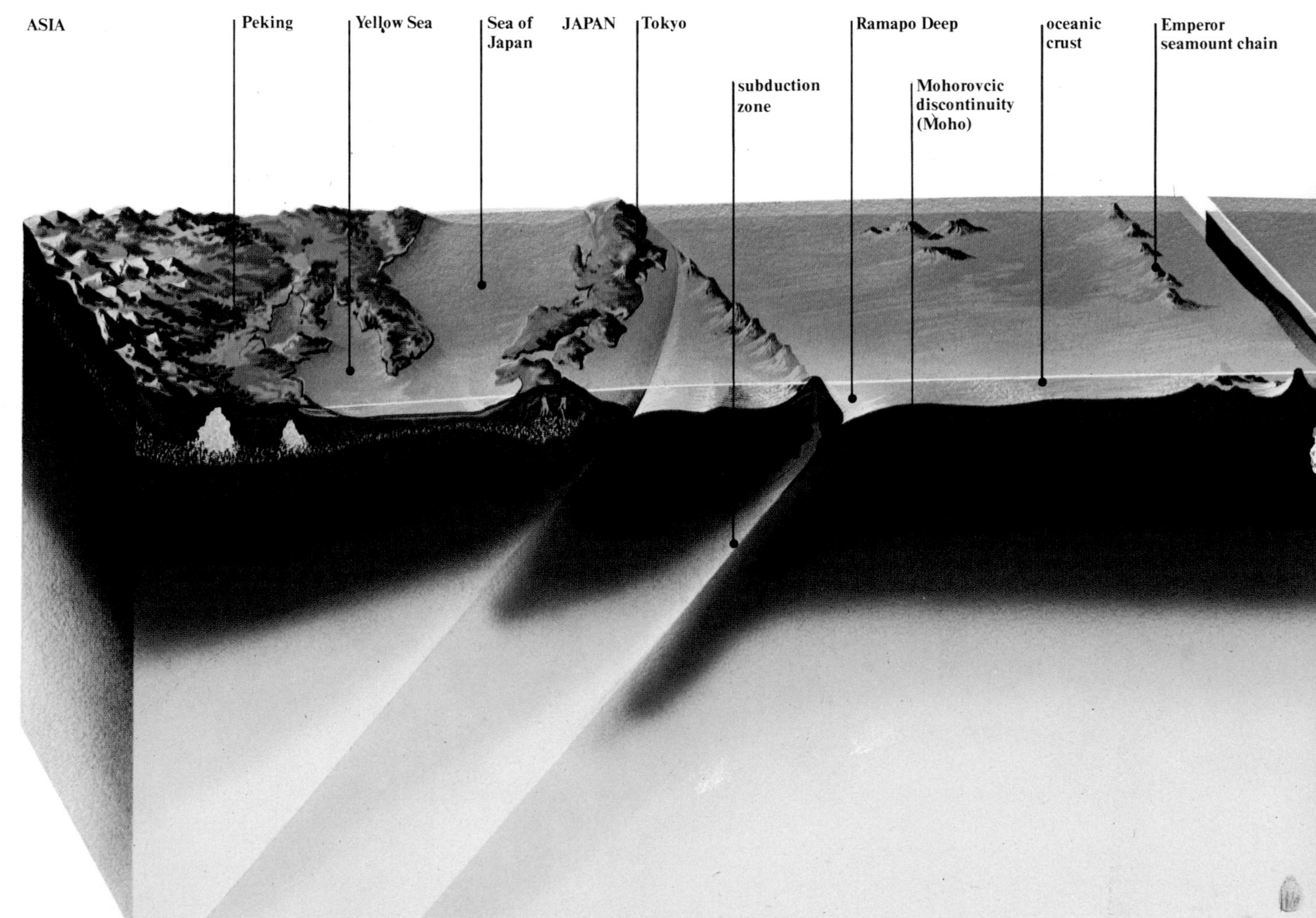

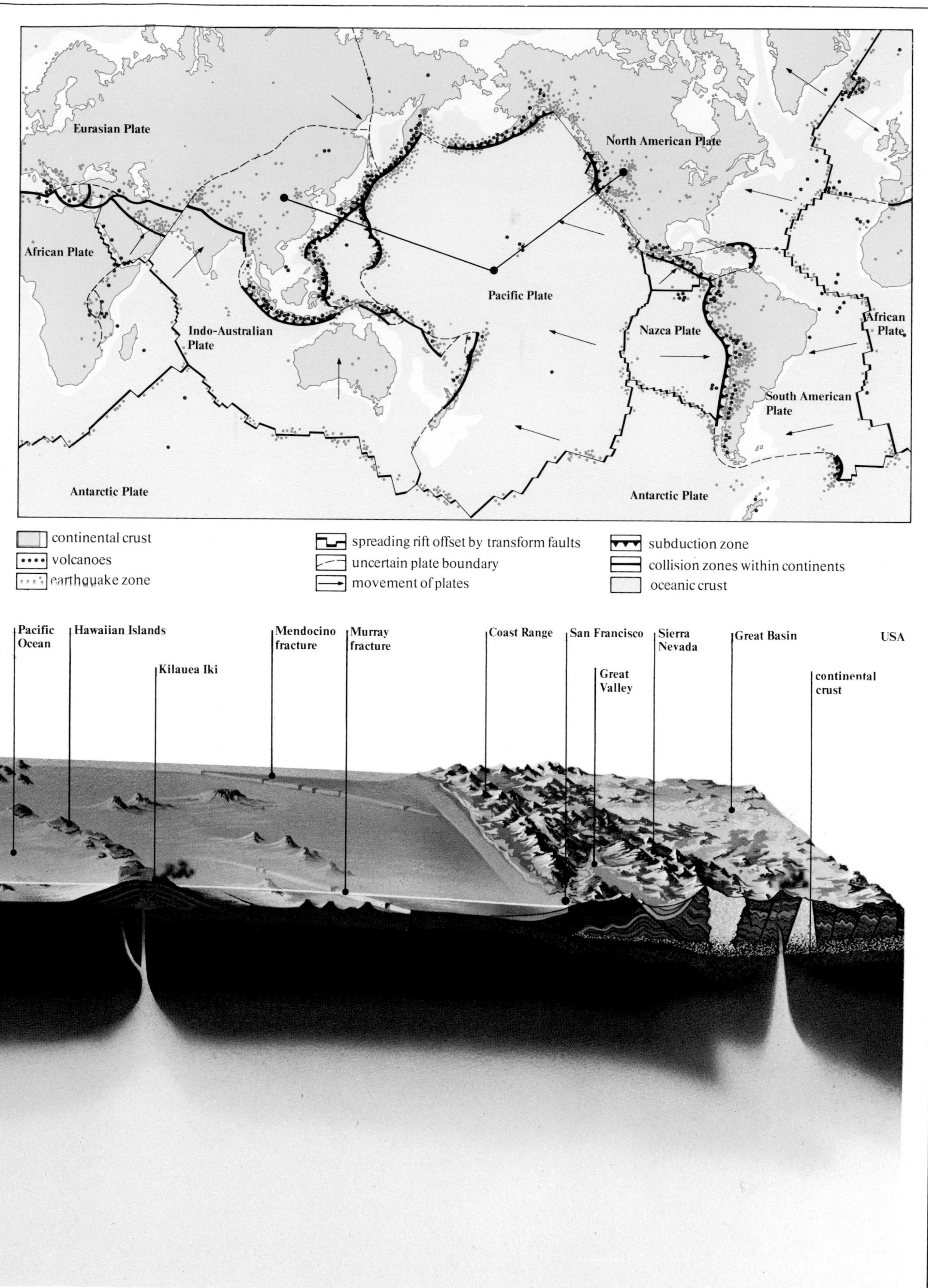
Eurasian Plate
North American Plate
African Plate
Pacific Plate
Indo-Australian Plate
Nazca Plate
African Plate
South American Plate
Antarctic Plate
Antarctic Plate
continental crust
volcanoes
earthquake zone
spreading rift offset by transform faults
uncertain plate boundary
movement of plates
subduction zone
collision zones within continents
oceanic crust
Pacific Ocean
Hawaiian Islands
Kilauea Iki
Mendocino fracture
Murray fracture
Coast Range
San Francisco
Great Valley
Sierra Nevada
Great Basin
USA
continental crust

Earthquakes are not exactly providers of material wealth in themselves, but mark by their rumblings the active processes which, going on continuously for millions and hundreds of millions of years, have built up the reserves on which civilization lives today. The key to this process of concentration can be seen most clearly today in the Red Sea, that 'baby' ocean which is now splitting two continents apart.

Like any other spreading ocean, the Red Sea is marked by the spine of a spreading ridge where new oceanic crust is being created. Underwater volcanism, earthquake activity and so on are commonplace features of such ridges, which are scarred by the deep faults that, underwater, become known as trenches or, prosaically, simply as 'deeps.' The Red Sea ridge is no exception, and the discovery of a series of deeps up the spine of that sea in the late 1960s, and their investigation (when not hampered by Arab/Israeli conflict) in the early 1970s helped to set the seal on the modern understanding of the basics of plate tectonics. And now with the basics of understanding laid down, the era of exploitation is at hand.

The year 1977 marked the time when the new science of geophysics 'came of age' in this respect, with the signing of a contract in Paris by the Red Sea Commission and the Argas company which opened the way for 'mining' the metal-rich sediments of the Red Sea deeps – sediments laid down by the key processes of tectonics.

Where the new sea floor is being created, metal-rich rocks and lava are brought to the surface and into contact with sea water; the result is that hot brine pools form in these 'deeps,' richly laden with dissolved salts of metals. The metallic salts are then laid down in sediments in the deeps to provide a rich source to be mined – in the Red Sea, some of these sediments contain 5.8 percent zinc, 0.9 percent copper and 110 grams of silver in every ton of dry material, enough to make the effort involved in extracting them thoroughly worthwhile. The first fault which is to be exploited, the Atlantis II Deep, is thought to contain 850 million tons of sediment, which should include 7 million tons of copper.

From this pioneering venture, geophysics and industry may well combine in the not too distant future to realize that age-old dream, extraction of minerals directly from sea water. Where this is likely to remain impracticable as far as ordinary sea water is concerned for many years to come, the extra richness of the brines in the Red Sea deeps makes the prospect that much more plausible, and brings it that much closer. And, of course, the exploitation of the Red Sea in this way is the beginning, not the end, of a new era in 'mining' the sea and sea bed.

If the Red Sea ridge can be exploited in this way, then surely one day the technique can be stretched to deal with the greater, but not insurmountable, problems of tapping the resources of other ocean ridges, such as the mid-Atlantic Ridge.

Another story which made headlines in 1977 concerned the discovery of 'underwater geysers' two miles (three kilometers) below the surface of the Pacific Ocean at the Galapagos Rift, a great crack in the sea floor running east-west for 1000 miles (1600 kilometers) near the Galapagos Islands.

This crack, too, is part of the great spreading ridge system which girdles the Earth, and it has been studied recently by instrument packages towed across the rift by the Research Vessel *Melville*, operated by the Scripps Institution in California. The evidence gathered during the *Melville's* survey shows that cold water flows down through cracks in the Earth's crust at the edges of the rift, comes into contact with hot molten rock at the site of the spreading activity, and gushes upward at the central split in the spine, laden with a rich burden of manganese, zinc, iron, nickel, cobalt and sulphur.

As well as helping geophysicists to pin down the processes by which deposits of such minerals were laid down in the past, this discovery could well be of practical benefit today. The processes are just the same as those operating in the Red Sea, which is already being exploited. And if a two-mile deep layer of ocean seems a not insignificant barrier to similar exploitation of the Galapagos Rift, the following tale serves to convince.

One of the most surprising discoveries made in recent years during surveys of the ocean bed was the existence of 'nodules' of manganese scattered here and there. These nodules are more or less spherical lumps, usually a few inches across but ranging up to giants weighing hundreds of pounds. The way in which they form is reminiscent of the development of a pearl around a piece of grit in an oyster – the layers of manganese are deposited, like onion skins, around some small piece of suitable material, often a pebble but in at least one recorded case a shark's tooth.

Once again, it has been Scripps Institution studies of the region near the Galapagos Rift that have confirmed beyond reasonable doubt that these nodules are built up from the richly laden waters near the sites of sea-floor spreading, where minerals are dissolved into the hot brines. In this case, though, the building process is rather laborious – a nodule grows by only a few millimeters in diameter over a period of a thousand years or more.

Manganese is a particularly rare element – a few deposits are known in Africa, India and the Soviet Union – and is particularly valuable in industry, where it forms a vital and irreplaceable component in the manufacture of the hardest steel. So it is worth developing ways to dredge up these nodules from the sea bed, even at great expense. The rewards could be astronomical, and this realization formed the background to one of the most curious stories of the 1970s.

If one has the right kind of imagination, it might seem fairly logical to set about extracting the wealth of these manganese nodules by using some kind of giant vacuum cleaner, or a scoop, to bring them to the surface. To do the job effectively, one would need a very special, and very expensive, ship. Hence the interest of the news-hounds of a few years back when they began to sniff out details of a *most* peculiar project being funded by one arm of the Howard Hughes organization.

The stories that leaked out about the building of the great *Glomar Explorer* in California were a classic of subterfuge. At first, the ship was reported to be a geophysical explorer (hence the name) along the lines of the *Glomar Challenger* but bigger and better. The *Challenger* has been responsible for some of the most important studies of the sea bed through the 1960s and 1970s, providing the cores, drilled from the ocean floor, which fleshed out the bones of the theory of plate tectonics. And the *Explorer* was being built by the same company as the *Challenger*. But would the Hughes' organization be interested in 'blue sky' – in this case, 'blue ocean' – research? The news-hounds smelled a rat and dug deeper, coming up with the beautifully planned cover story that the *Explorer* was really designed to scoop up those manganese nodules, stealing a technological march on everybody else in the world and bringing a rich new source of revenue to its owners.

The *Glomar Explorer*, the Howard Hughes deep-sea research vessel, whose first task was to raise a wrecked Soviet nuclear submarine.

These diagrams explain the formation of the mid-Atlantic ridge. The continents of the two Americas (left) and Europe-Africa (right) are split by rock welling up from within the earth's core. As the rift widens, the rock emerging at the ridge runs away to left and right, bearing away both the continental plates and the up-welling rocky ridges.

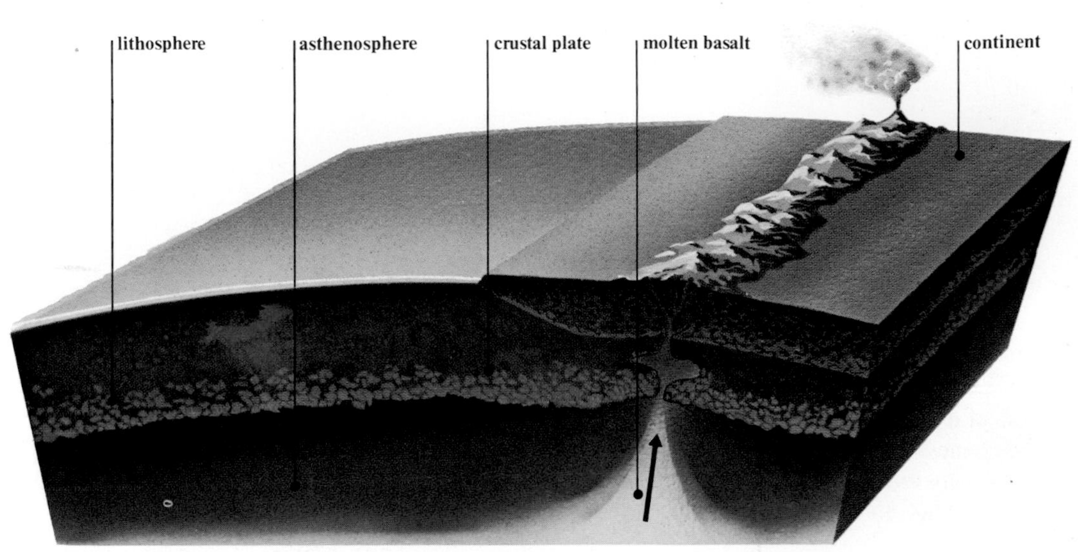

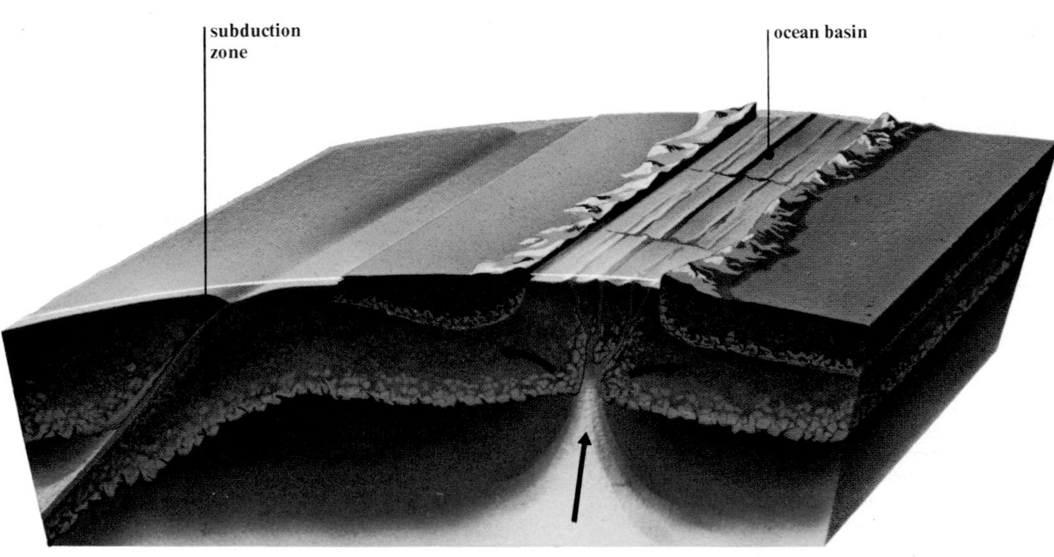

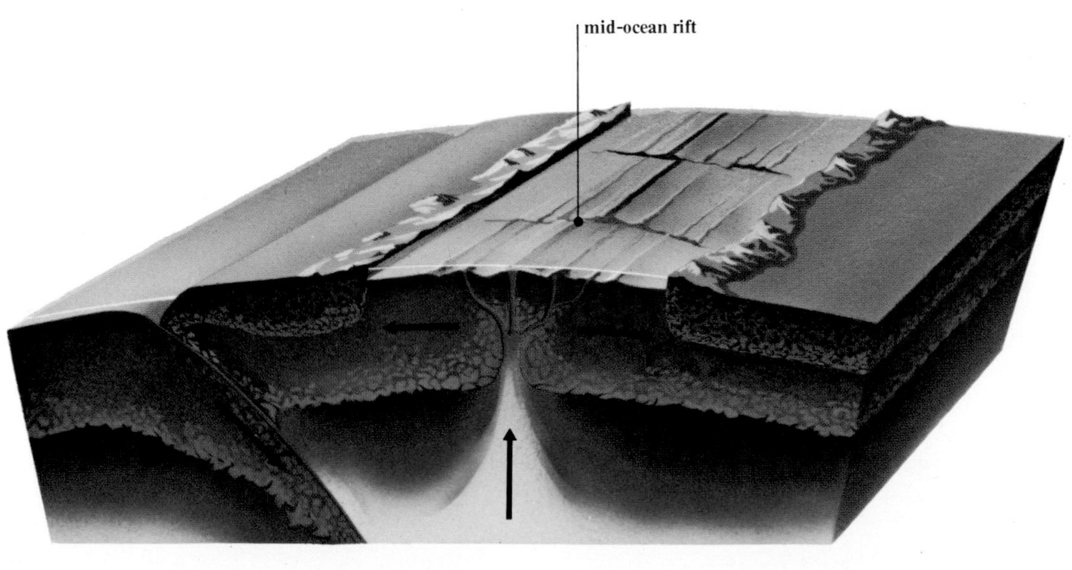

The steam of a geothermal plant in Iceland exemplifies the power that is already being won from the energy released by the heat of the earth's interior.

This story had all the hallmarks of the truth – it fitted in with Hughes' notorious reputation for secrecy, and more significantly with the plausible business practice of spending money to make money.

But the reporters were all wrong; the nesting layers of stories and subterfuge still concealed the real truth behind the construction of the *Glomar Explorer*, a truth which only became clear after it had traveled on to the high seas and carried out its true mission – to recover the remains of a Soviet submarine that had sunk in the deep Pacific.

The story, when the true facts finally became known, caused a political furore which is of no concern here. But even then the tale had another ironic twist to unfold, a happy ending which seems likely to benefit the world's geophysicists.

In March 1977 Earth scientists meeting at Woods Hole in Massachusetts outlined their proposals for the next decade of deep sea research following the triumphant success of the work of the *Glomar Challenger*. What they needed was a bigger ship, able to drill in deeper water, to carry out the logical next stage in the exploration of planet Earth. Such a vessel would be cripplingly expensive – at least $100 million to build. But it just so happened that the geophysicists knew of a vessel that could be converted to do the job for just half that sum – the *Glomar Explorer*.

So the wheel turns full circle. It remains to be seen whether even $50 million, plus running costs, can be obtained for a further decade of ocean exploration, but the present first stirrings of economic success in exploitation of the resources discovered by the work of *Glomar Challenger* and others should tip the balance in favor of the new program. And then, who knows, the 1980s might see the converted *Explorer* actually fulfilling its originally spurious assignment – dredging up manganese nodules.

But however the wheel of fate turns for the *Glomar Explorer*, the intermission for international skullduggery has allowed other dredging projects, legitimate from the outset, to get in on the act. Belgium's Union Minière company is involved in trials for a deep-sea dredging vessel, *Deepsea Miner II*, about to begin mining operations (in 1978) in the Pacific some 1100 miles (1760 kilometers) southwest of San Diego; at least one other system, developed in the US, began trials late in 1977, and the French are already talking about a 'second generation' system in which the deep sea 'mining' (collection of nodules) would be carried out automatically by unmanned submarine dredgers.

Warmth from the Earth's interior, reaching up through thin regions of crust but stopping short of volcanic activity as conventionally

Volcanic wealth: A sulphur mine (top) at 6000 meters (18,000 feet) – the highest mine in the world on Aucanquilcha Volcano, Chile; and the ancient volcano of Cerro Rici, Potosia, Bolivia, which has been heavily mined for silver since the 16th century.

understood is particularly important in the formation of oil deposits – and an understanding of continental drift helps to explain why present day oil reserves are located where they are, as well as suggesting new sites for oil exploration.

The organic processes which produce the hydrocarbon reserves such as oil and natural gas depend on a lavish supply of organic material, vegetable or animal remains, conveniently swept up by river systems and deposited in deltas, shallow lakes or inshore coastal regions. The deposits can then be covered up by sediments which slowly form into layers or rock, while the organic remains are converted into hydrocarbon fuels by the action of bacteria. This takes a very long time, genuinely 'geological' time, well up into the tens and hundreds of millions of years. And this is where an understanding of plate tectonics helps in locating oil reserves today.

To make anything worthwhile in the way of an oil reservoir, the amount of organic debris laid down in the sediments must be large, and that means that the sites of potential oil reserves must start out in essentially tropical conditions, where the rich variety of life leaves its remains to be swept down into the great river deltas. So hydrocarbon reserves originate in tropical conditions – not just oil and gas reserves, but coal as well. But today, of course, such reserves are located as far from the tropics as Antarctica, Alaska and the North Sea – a discovery which, even without the modern theory of plate tectonics, is very powerful circumstantial evidence for the occurrence of some form of continental drift.

The trick, then, for any oil company or government anxious to tap new sources of fuel is to locate regions of the globe which *were* in the tropics long ago, and which might therefore contain the necessary richness of organic remains. Then, the more traditional techniques of the petroleum geologist can be called in to identify the small percentage of such regions that has the right structure for first forming and then trapping the chemical hydrocarbons.

One feature which helps the process of formation of these deposits along is the application of gentle heat. Not too much, so that the hydrocarbons evaporate, but a little to stimulate the organic processes of conversion and to encourage the products to migrate through porous rocks and gather in concentrations below domes of non-porous rock, ready to be tapped by the oil man's drill. Such warmth occurs commonly in regions where the Earth's crust has been stretched slightly, without quite cracking apart to form a new spreading ocean.

The opening of the North Atlantic, beginning rather less than 200 million years ago, provides the classic example in geophysics of how this stretching occurs. Early on in the break-up of the preceding supercontinent, rifts developed down three lines: the present Atlantic spreading ridge, the Barents Sea and the North Sea. In due course, the mid-Atlantic Ridge dominated, and the incipient spreading at the other sites halted, but not before the Earth's crust had been stretched and thinned a little locally.

With other conditions also right for the formation of hydrocarbon deposits, this thinning added the finishing touch and helped to ensure that warmth from the Earth's interior would do the necessary baking job. The fact that the rich reserves of oil under the North Sea were found almost by accident in the 1960s is simply one of the ironies of nature – the explorers were just a few years ahead of the theory's development, but if they had not been, then surely in the early 1970s drilling would have got underway under the impetus of the implications of the new developments of geophysics. And it does not take too much geophysical genius to guess, with the benefit of North Sea success as well as the geophysical theory, that there should be equally good pickings just next door, in that other region of stretch which did not quite become an ocean, the Barents Sea.

The ways in which metallic ores and economically valuable solid minerals are – or were – deposited also depend in part on activity within the earth, in this case largely volcanic. The results have been the sources of the great riches made by those few prospectors who have struck lucky over the past hundred years or so, and still provide great quantities of such vital materials as gold, silver, copper and sulphur. Taking these in order as case studies, one can see just how volcanoes concentrate these resources – for it is the *concentration* that really matters to commercial exploiters. Sea water contains gold and other minerals, but only in extremely thin concentrations (except in certain hot brines), and although the ordinary crust of the continents contains gold it is only at a concentration of about 0·004 parts in a million, which hardly makes its extraction a tempting commercial prospect. But in the Witwatersrand gold-field of South Africa, this concentration is increased more than a thousandfold, to 7 parts per million, which makes all the difference.

Many factors contribute to the formation of ore bodies – reserves where the concentration of a particular valuable element rises high enough to make commercial exploitation worthwhile – and as well as the heating and concentrating effect of volcanism, there is the sedimentation which lays down material in the first place, transportation by various processes including volcanism, and, by no means least, the weathering away of rock after all this activity is over to expose the concentrated ore bodies. Gold is unusual in that it is found as an element in some ore bodies – most minerals are chemical compounds in which valuable elements are bound up with more common elements such as carbon, oxygen and silicon.

In his excellent book *Volcanoes*, Peter Francis quotes the example of the Cripple Creek gold deposits in Colorado, where all these formation processes have played a part. The gold found there is in the roots of an old volcano, about 660 yards (600 meters) of which have weathered away to expose the various 'pipes' and 'necks' which once fed fluid magma into the active craters above. The gold ore occurs in sheets and 'veins,' which cut across the basaltic material left behind by the volcanic activity, and range from hairline threads up to twisted sheets more than 11 yards (10 meters) across. The gold from one pipe alone, discovered in 1915, yielded 1,800,000 tons.

Silver deposits formed by similar volcanic processes have also provided bonanzas for the miners of the past 100 years, and one of the classic examples is the Comstock Lode in Nevada, where the discovery of rich silver deposits played a big part in the opening up of the American west. Another rich silver deposit associated with an eroded old volcano played a significant part in the exploitation of South America after the Spanish conquest of Peru in the sixteenth century. The Bolivian 'hill of Silver' (Cerro Rici) contributed in no small measure to the Spanish treasury.

Meanwhile, South America is known today for another reserve as vital as silver to the world's economy: copper. Volcanic activity in the Chilean Andes has built up vast reserves of copper, a metal so important to the electrical machinery that plays such a big part in modern civilization that it can be mined at a profit even in deposits where the concentration is only about half a percent.

In this illustrious company of riches, one gemstone must be mentioned – and that stone, diamond, forms *only* through the effects of volcanic activity in the fissures found in the rock, kimberlite, fissures through which molten magma once flowed. These kimberlite pipes do not always contain diamonds, and it has long proved something of an embarrassment to geologists to explain why some held diamonds while others did not. Equally puzzling was the evidence that although involved in the violent processes of volcanism, the contents of the pipes had never been exposed directly to the very great extremes of pressure which are necessary to make diamond crystals – chips of compressed carbon – artificially.

Both these puzzles seem to have been resolved by comparison with, of all things, the wake produced by a ship's propellor as it

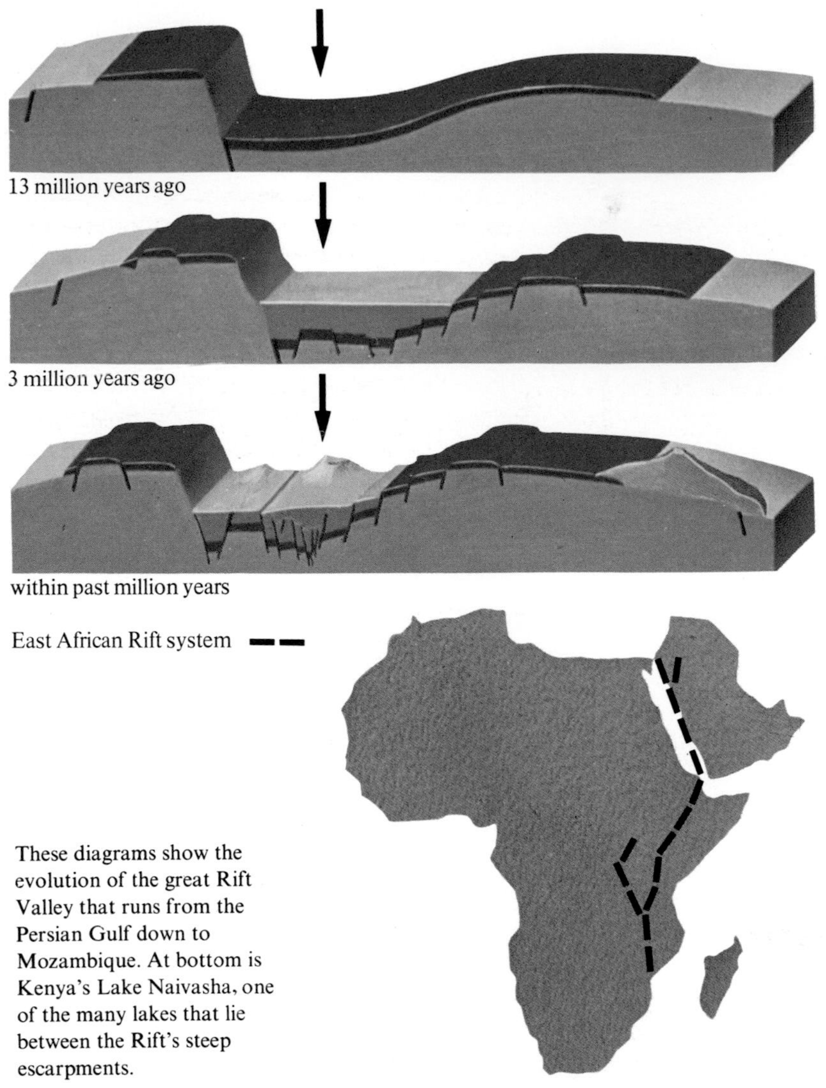

These diagrams show the evolution of the great Rift Valley that runs from the Persian Gulf down to Mozambique. At bottom is Kenya's Lake Naivasha, one of the many lakes that lie between the Rift's steep escarpments.

whisks through the water. In liquids that contain dissolved gases, such as magma or sea water, turbulant stirring of the liquid can produce a process known as *cavitation*, which among other things is responsible for the pitting of ships' propellers and the internal parts of pumps. What happens is that pressure at some point in the liquid first drops, releasing a bubble of gas, then rises again so that the bubble collapses. At the center of the collapsing bubble, very high pressures can be produced locally for a short time. Motion of an object like a ship's propeller through sea water is an ideal way to produce cavitation; now, it seems that cavitation can also occur in the formation of kimberlite pipes, if the conditions are right. The fluid magma entering the cracks in the rock contains a great deal of dissolved carbon dioxide which leaves its trace behind on the solid pipes in the form of widely dispersed deposits of various carbonates. If the pipe is partly obstructed, then as the magma flows past, cavitation is inevitable; if there is no obstruction, or none of the right size, cavitation does not occur. This is why some kimberlite pipes contain diamonds while others do not.

Typical pipes of this kind run vertically for several kilometers and are a few tens of meters wide; where the pressure changes as the pipe is constricted and opens out again, cavitation can occur producing local pressures of more

than 1000 kilobars – and the pressure needed to make artificial diamonds is only 100 kilobars ('only' here is a relative term; ordinary atmospheric pressure is just about one bar, and one kilobar is a thousand bars). The pressure only lasts for a few thousandths of a second, but even that is much longer than is needed to produce artificial diamonds.

Until the cavitation technique can be applied in the laboratory, volcanic sites will remain the only source of large, perfect diamonds – and only the volcanic sites where kimberlite pipes occur, with only some of these pipes containing any diamonds. With diamonds important in industry and for drill teeth, as well as to provide a show of wealth for the few, this is still one area in which volcanic activity has made a unique contribution to our society.

Sulphur may seem a less exciting substance than gold, copper, silver or diamonds, but it is of enormous importance to the chemical industry, and is produced in such copious quantities by volcanoes that it can hardly be ignored in any mention of the commercial value of these fiery reservoirs of wealth. Ironically though, in spite of the association of sulphur with volcanoes (and hell-fire under the name 'brimstone'), and the undeniable existence of huge deposits of sulphur produced by volcanic activity directly, there are other reserves of the stuff so ready to mine that volcanoes hardly get considered where the world markets are concerned.

The biggest source of sulphur for the world market is the southern part of the US where the deposits are believed to have had a biological origin (reminiscent of the origin of oil and gas deposits). But there are a couple of large volcanic sulphur mines in Chile, which have been described by Peter Francis among others. One of these mines is worth noting as the highest working mine in the world, reaching up to 6600 yards (6000 meters) above sea level and lying in the core of a volcano which is still slightly active, producing sulphurous fumes which add to the burden of the miners working at such extreme altitude. Hardly surprisingly, the combination of hard work, high altitude and a lacing of fumes results in a short life expectancy for the miners, Indians from the Bolivian high plateau.

The final benefit that can be derived from volcanic activity is energy. Geothermal power has long been tapped in some places, such as Iceland, where geysers and hot springs bring the energy of the Earth's interior heat into prominent visibility at the Earth's surface. But these obvious sources of virtually free energy are far outnumbered by the sites where water laden strata lie over hot bulges of magma which have pushed upward but not broken through to the surface; it would not be difficult to drill into these hot spots, from which the water would then issue as steam as pressure was released. Deep in the rocks water is kept liquid by the high pressure even when its temperature reaches 260°C (500°F). And, in principle, this idea can be taken one step further, when even *dry* 'hot spots' can be drilled, and water pumped in one end while steam is extracted from the other.

Studies by a team at Los Alamos Scientific Laboratory in New Mexico have already taken this science-fiction-like idea into the world of practical reality, by drilling a bore-hole to a depth of 1.8 miles (three kilometers) where the rock below New Mexico reaches a temperature of 200°C (424°F), about three times more than is usual for rock at that depth elsewhere in the world. Water pumped down this bore-hole caused the rock to crack into many fissures through which water and steam could then percolate and become superheated. With a second bore-hole then drilled into the fracture zone, 90 percent of the water being pumped down returned to the surface, with a flow sufficient to produce a power generation of several megawatts – much more than the energy involved in setting up the cycle. The next step, drilling to 2.5 miles (four kilometers) depth and 250°C (482°F), should produce from one pair of bore-holes an effective 50 megawatt power supply, comparing well with conventional power stations.

A better – if risky – source might be to tap the energies of active volcanoes directly (provided one is prepared to take the chance of setting off more energetic production than one wants in explosive form!). Scientists at the University of Hawaii have suggested seriously that natural reservoirs of superheated water in the rocks around volcanoes could be tapped for steam power by suitably sited bore-holes, and have even gone so far as to suggest pouring cold water into the fiery mouth of an Etna or a Vesuvius to produce steam. Perhaps the world is not yet that desperate for power – but even such way-out speculation helps to remind the inhabitants of this planet that inside the Earth is a vast reservoir of energy in the form of heat, which could prove far more valuable in the long run than coal or oil – and which, in addition, is non-polluting.

INTO THE GREAT RIFT

About 20 miles west of Nairobi stand the Ngong Hills (below). From their ridge is a startling view (right) – an immense plain stretching into the distance. Thirty miles away rises a colossal wall, the Nguruman Scarp, blue in the haze. This is just one section of Africa's Great Rift Valley, itself a section of a 1500-mile scar between the Red Sea and Lake Manyara, Tanzania, along which the earth is literally being torn apart at the seams. In Africa, the Rift begins in the Danakil Depression on the Red Sea, narrowing to a 30-mile cut, dotted with soda lakes and volcanoes, as it plunges southwards, through Lake Rudolf, past the Ngong Hills and on to Lake Manyara. An offshoot, known as the Western Rift, branches off along the Zaire-Uganda border, swinging southwards through Lakes Albert and Tanganyika.

This split in the earth's crust is such a huge feature that its very existence was not suspected until the 1890s when a young Scottish geologist, John Walter Gregory, discovered that the rocks on opposing walls matched up, and suggested that they formed a previously unrecognized land form: 'For this type of valley I suggest the name of Rift Valley, using the term rift in the sense of a relatively narrow space due to subsidence between parallel fractures.' As a result of his insight, the valley is sometimes still referred to as the Gregory Rift.

Since Gregory's day, geologists have dated the activity that formed the Rift. Its formation began 200 million years ago when Pangaea began to break up. The rocks began to pull apart and a central section dropped. Since then magma has continually risen through volcanic vents to fill the space made by the ever widening walls of the Rift.

Some geologists speak of the Great Rift Valley as 'an aborted ocean.' There, but for the grace of unfathomable underground forces, they say, should have gone a large piece of Africa east of the Rift, floating off like Madagascar. If this had happened, salt water would have filled the Rift until it resembled the Red Sea. The eastern half of Ethiopia, all of Somalia, and half of Kenya and Tanzania would have become a large offshore island. In the event a new sea was not formed. But the valley is still young: eventually, tens of millions of years hence, it will become an inlet of the Indian Ocean.

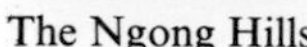

The Ngong Hills

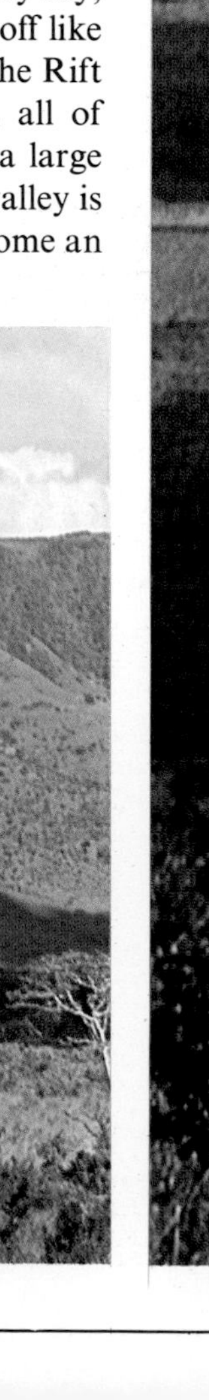

A view across the Valley from the top of the Ngong Hills

The 9000-foot dome of Ol Doinyo Lengai (Masai: 'Mountain of God') bears witness to countless eruptions. The last was in 1966.

Magma seethes in the crater of Nyirangongo, Zaire, in the Western Rift. The volcano has been active, with few interruptions, since 1935.

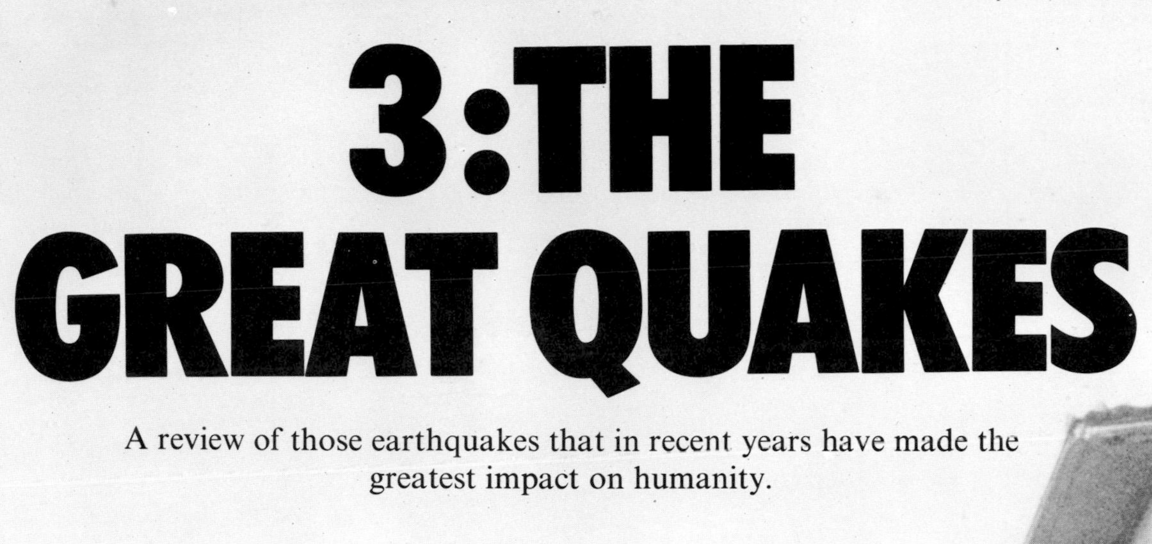

3: THE GREAT QUAKES

A review of those earthquakes that in recent years have made the greatest impact on humanity.

An apartment block ruined by the Bucharest earthquake, 4 March 1975

Any discussion of the great quakes of the recent past must start with the San Francisco earthquake of 1906, a disaster so tremendous and so relatively recent, that it has become part of human folklore. The disaster also serves as an archetypal case study in two very important respects. First, the quake occurred exactly where two of the great tectonic plates that make up the Earth's crust rub shoulders. Nothing was known of plate tectonics in 1906, of course, but today one can see why California should be prone to earthquakes, and one can be certain that further quakes, equally as severe as the great disaster of 1906, are going to recur, quite probably before the end of this century. The second classic feature of the destruction of San Francisco has nothing to do with the direct effects of the shaking Earth, but highlights a feature not often realized by anyone who has not experienced a quake. The actual shaking of the Earth itself was *not* the main direct cause of trouble. The greatest damage and difficulty was caused by the fire which followed.

In any earthquake (except the very largest disruptions of the Earth's crust) the greatest threat to cities and people is the threat of fire, and this remains true to the present day. Perhaps the second greatest hazard today, especially in California, is the threat of flooding from the many dams and artifical lakes high in the mountains above cities (such as Los Angeles), built dangerously close to the zone of greatest earthquake risk. Indeed, for once, a tribute should perhaps be paid by the scientists to the movie industry, for the disaster epic *Earthquake* struck precisely the right note in terms of the awesome combination of fire and flood as the secondary but most damaging consequences of the next California quake disaster.

Getting back to 1906, however, the comparison can be made dramatically in financial terms. Loss of life, even in this folk-memory disaster, was actually less than one thousand –

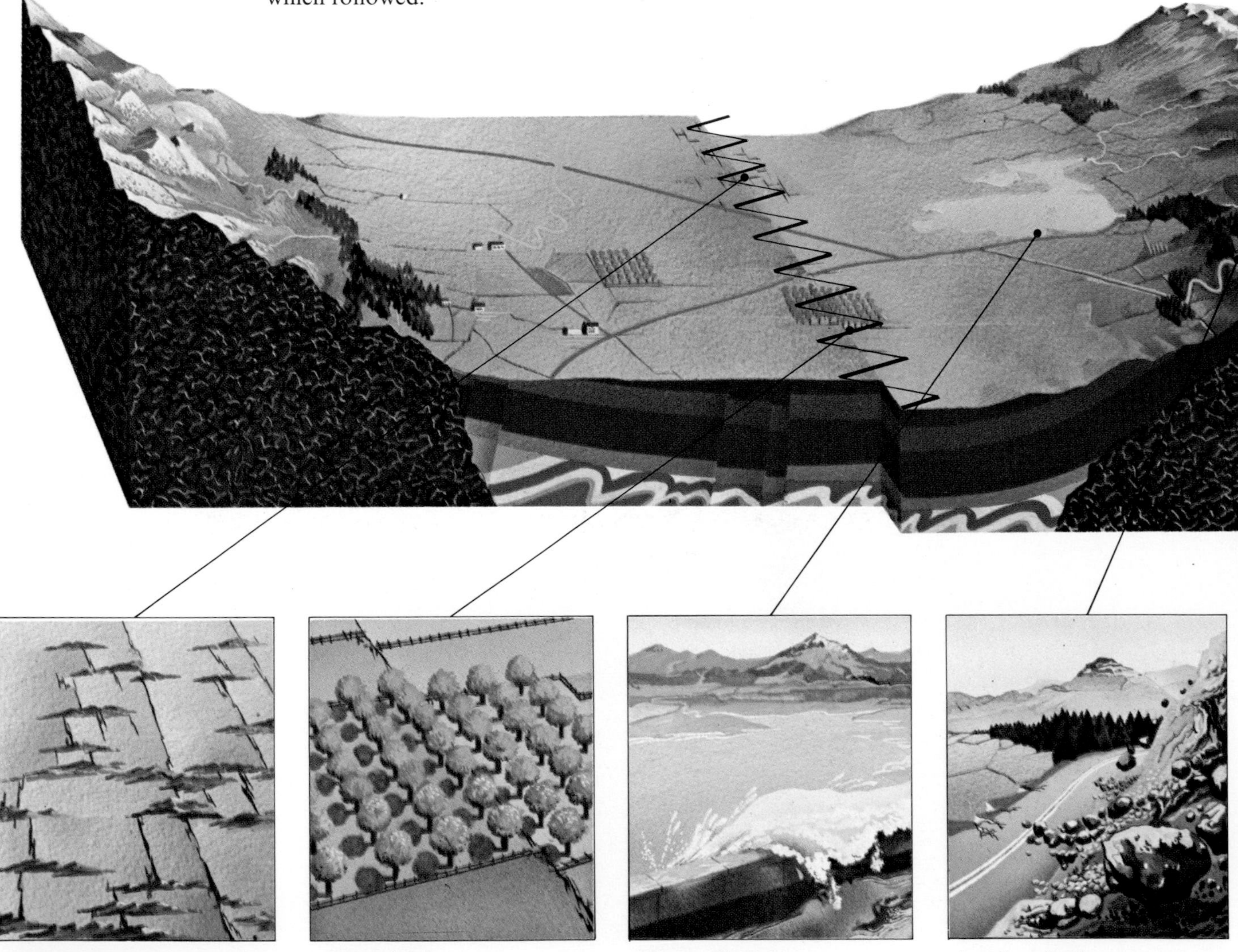

A field cracks open

A lateral shift

Lake overflowing

A rock avalanche

but as much by luck as judgment. The financial loss was about $20 million from the direct effects of the quake – but about four *hundred* million dollars through fire. The quake lasted only a couple of minutes – long enough to wreck the cities' new $6 million City Hall, but not long in human terms; the fire raged for three days before being brought under control, devouring 30 schools, 80 churches and convents, the homes of about 250,000 people and almost 500 lives.

Among those lives lost to the fire one has to include the grim cases of mercy killings, at least two of which were fully documented by eyewitnesses at the time. One man, for example, was trapped in the remains of a building, unable to escape as the wall of fire approached in spite of the efforts to help made by a soldier at the scene. After repeated desperate pleas from the victim, the soldier finally complied with his last request – to shoot him through the head before the fire took hold. Other shootings occurred as law and order began to break down and looters sought what they could in the rubble of the city. Attempting to prevent the spread of disorder, the Mayor appointed a vigilante group of 'responsible' armed citizens to keep the peace. Unfortunately, these citizens proved more than a little trigger happy in some cases, and two 'criminals' were shot down for insulting ladies in the Golden Gate Park. As the military moved in to take control there were other isolated clashes with vigilantes reluctant to yield their own short-lived importance; the vigilantes were told that they would be shot if they failed to give up their weapons. Another lesson learned the hard way to be born in mind at future disasters: arms and the control of law and order are best left to trained and disciplined men, or the end product may be more trouble than the situation which is supposed to be in need of control.

And the hardest lesson of all, with repercussions not felt just by the citizens of San

This diagramatic profile of an earthquake shows the variety of effects a single shock of magnitude 7.0 on the Richter Scale can cause. In this case the shock spreads from a single fault movement which causes rupturing in the ground and spreads shock waves up to a hundred miles.

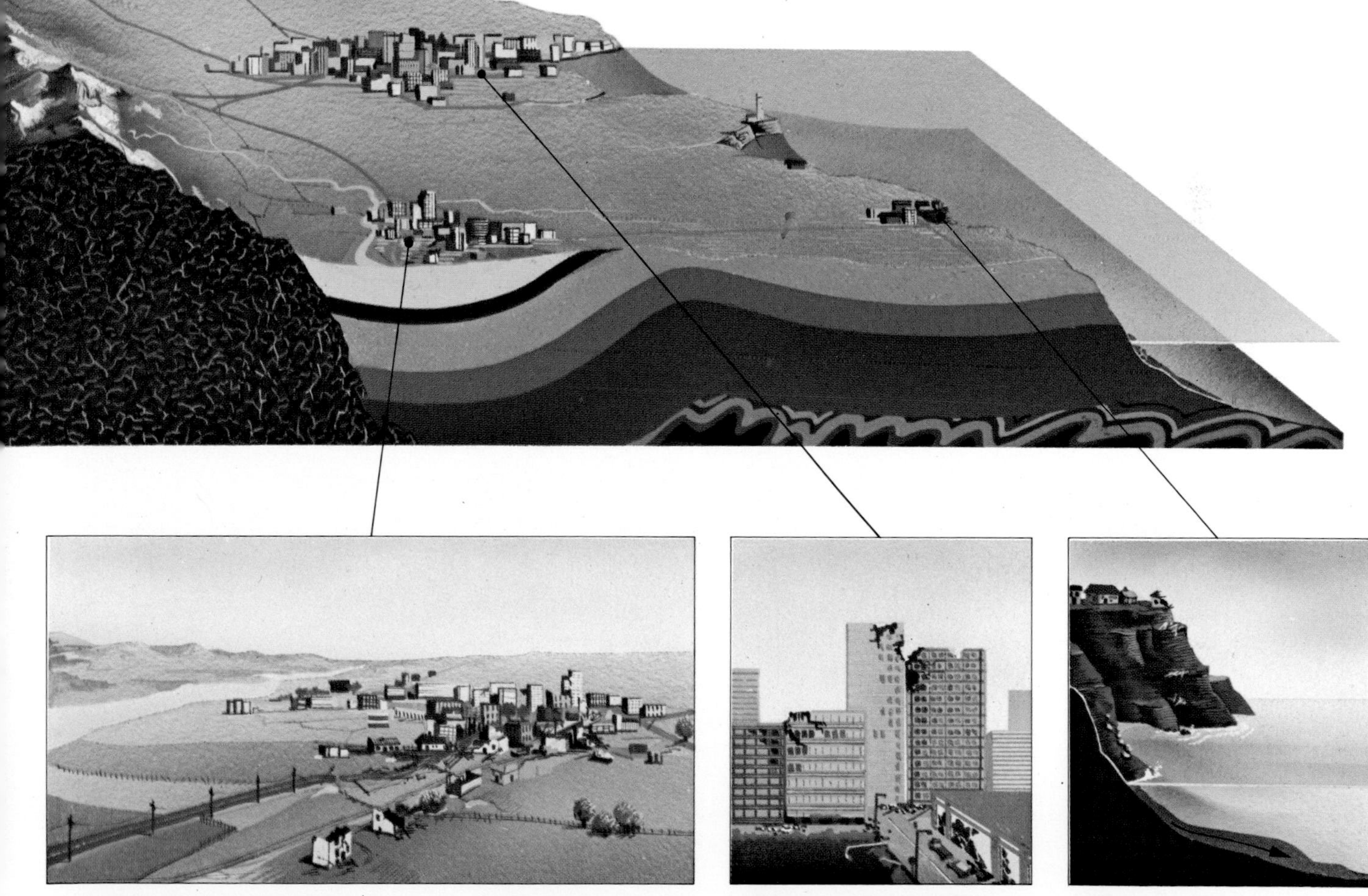

Local devastation of buildings

High rise buildings tumble

Cliffs tumble; sea floor drops

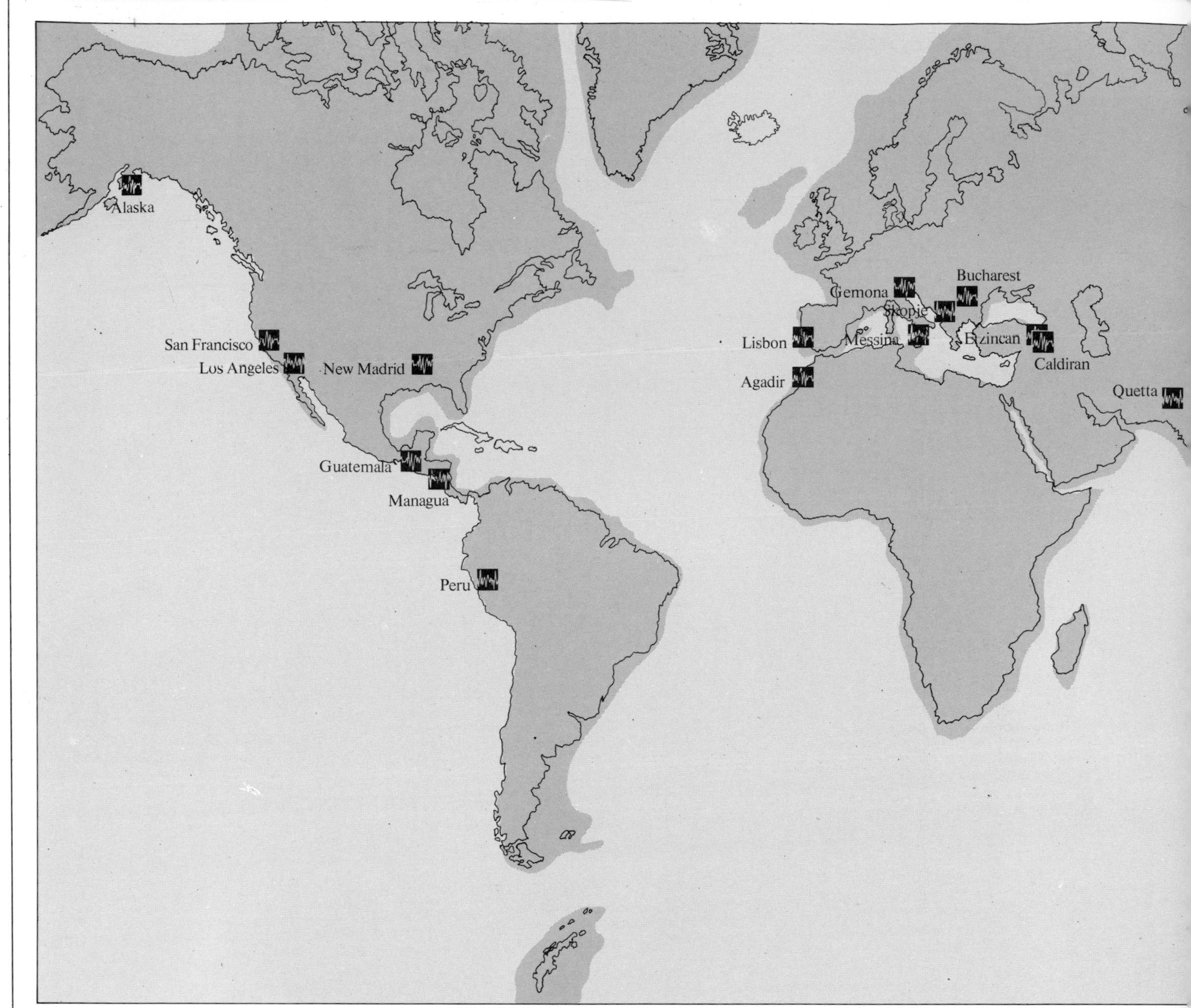

Francisco but by the luckless victims of later earthquakes, was that insurance companies, in many cases, simply could not cope with a disaster of this magnitude. As the companies crashed into insolvency, people whose homes and possessions were destroyed found that their insurance policies were no longer worth the paper on which they were printed. Surviving companies solved this problem in future policies – they added small print which stated that the effects of earthquakes were excluded from cover – as many a victim of later disasters found to his horror. Even so, some companies *did* pay out on the ensuing claims, and not least among these was Lloyds of London which enhanced its reputation at the forefront of insurance not just by paying out but by offering to insure new property in the California risk zone. Just how wise that commitment was should become apparent during the next decade or so.

Astonishingly, San Francisco itself was rebuilt within three years and now stands on its beautiful site around the Bay, still straddling the San Andreas Fault and destined for more bumps as the Pacific and North American plates grind past one another. For people who have now lived out their lives happily in this danger zone with no quake disaster, the gamble has paid off. But for those living there now, the name of the game is simply Russian roulette.

If the San Francisco disaster proved remarkably sparing of human lives, the next major quake disaster made up for this cosmic oversight. In 1923 Japan was hit by a seismic shake-up that killed more than 140,000 people. The magnitude of this earthquake was 8.2, very close in size to the 1906 California earthquake. Once again the chief agent of disaster was fire – spread disastrously on this occasion partly because the quake struck just

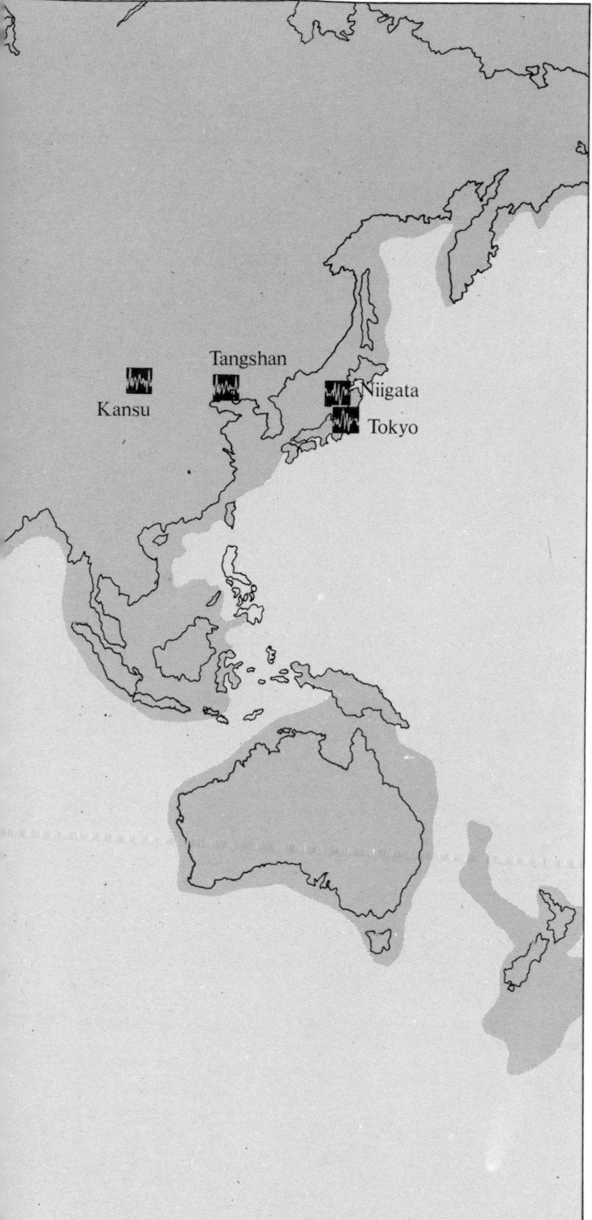

EARTHQUAKES: THE TOP TWENTY

Date	Place	Est. Deaths
1755	Lisbon, Portugal	6,000
1811	New Madrid, Missouri	Few known
1866	Peru and Ecuador	25,000
1906	San Francisco	500
1908	Messina, Italy	160,000
1920	Kansu, China	180,000
1923	Tokyo, Japan	143,000
1935	Quetta, Pakistan	60,000
1939	Erzincan, Turkey	40,000
1960	Agadir, Morocco	12,000
1963	Skopje, Yugoslavia	1,000
1964	Niigata, Japan	250
1964	Anchorage, Alaska	100
1971	Los Angeles	50
1972	Managua, Nicaragua	12,000
1975	Bucharest, Rumania	1,500
1976	Guatemala	23,000
1976	Gemona, Italy	1,000
1976	Caldiran, Turkey	8,000
1976	Tangshan, China	500,000

Of the 50,000 annual earthquakes which can be felt without the aid of instruments, about 100 do some damage. Great ones occur about once a year. At left is a list of some of the greatest.

before noon on 1 September pitching hot stoves on which midday meals were being prepared against the inflammable materials of houses and furniture.

The cities of Yokohama and Tokyo were virtually destroyed in the ensuing conflagration which developed into a fire storm. As hot air from the inferno expanded and rose upward, fresh air swept in as powerful winds at ground level, fanning the flames to furnace heat. As the final blow from nature against humanity, a *tsunami* (tidal wave) associated with the earthquake swept the shore. This time the fire lasted for 'only' two days – but it stopped because it had raged so fiercely that nothing was left to burn, not because firemen had brought it under control. Of 134 fires centered in Tokyo, only 23 were extinguished by firemen.

In Yokohama 5 percent of the cities' population died – one person in every 20. Oil storage tanks in the harbor were ruptured, spreading their contents on the water, where ships were confronted by a wall of flame.

The description of a Russian writer, Petroff Skitaretz records the sensation of this earthquake: 'We were moving to Nakamura on the Bluff at Yokohama, . . . down below lay Yokohama like a busy ant-hill, trains running, people buying and selling on the streets, sluggish boats in the canals, and ships far and near in the blue bay rocking against the shore of a prosperous city. . . .

'We walked in the middle of the road, followed by the man pulling the cart. Then suddenly, very near the Bluff, I thought I heard the sound of an approaching train. I was surprised, for I knew no train ran near there. I was about to mention it to my wife, but there was no time. From somewhere I heard the roaring as of a wild animal, and a sudden fierce wind came up and bent the branches of the trees like a bow. The sound like an underground train came now from directly under our feet, seemingly some pent up, awful energy seeking escape. The angry roaring increased, an enraged shaking was coming upon us. The ground began to move, groaning and yanking us back and forth with the mad speed and frantic energy of a lunatic. We felt as though we were about to be torn to pieces, and the great earth was trying to shake off everything on it. We seemed to be grains shaken in a sieve. We could not stand and fell in opposite directions, but struggled together against a hedge at the roadside which we

grasped.

'I looked around. Everything was snapping and cracking, houses and stone walls we had just passed were down, and in front a one-storey wooden house moved for a few seconds more and then shook down . . . All of these things happened in five or six minutes, and in those few minutes Yokohama and Tokyo were doomed.'

Once again, though, the shattered ruins were rebuilt, in spite of the insurance problems, and once again hundreds of thousands of people are today settled seemingly happily in a major earthquake danger zone.

These two shots show the town of Yungay, Peru, before (left) and after (right) an earthquake released a wall of ice, boulders and mud in 1970, killing 20,000 people.

TOKYO: DEATH AT NOON

On 1 September 1923, at 11.58 and 44 seconds, Tokyo and the nearby port of Yokohama fell to one of the most destructive earthquakes ever recorded. The shocks continued throughout the day but added little to the original catastrophe.

At one-and-a-half minutes to noon most Japanese families were preparing their midday meals. The shock pitched over countless stoves, setting fire to hundreds of tinder-box houses – specially designed to ride out earthquakes or collapse easily without damaging the occupants. It was the fire that proved the greatest agent of destruction (left). At the Honjo Clothing Depot, 7000 were burnt to death almost instantaneously by the whirlpool of fire. They were the victims of a fire storm; as the air above the city became heated, it rose, creating a vacuum which drew in air from all sides at hurricane strength. There were gusts of 150 mph with the heat of a blast furnace. Trees were wrenched out of the ground. 'An 18-year-old girl came along,' recalled a police sergeant, 'rolling along like a ball.'

The total death toll was about 60,000 – 25,000 of them burnt beyond recognition. Up the coast, a *tsunami* swept in to add to the destruction. West of Yokohama the land rose seven and a half feet. Elsewhere it sank five and a half feet.

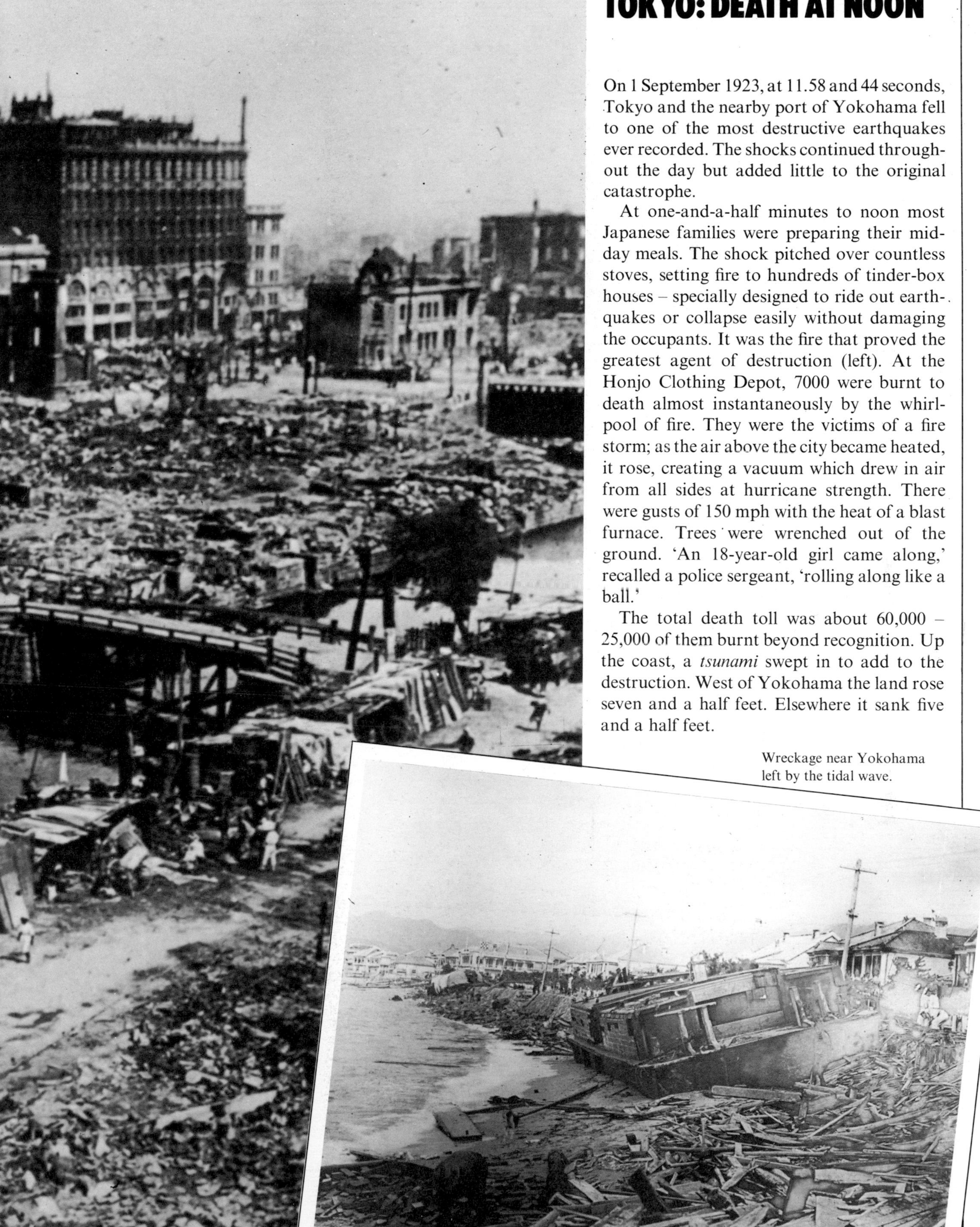

Wreckage near Yokohama left by the tidal wave.

A few days after the earthquake and fire, a Japanese family helps begin the task of clearing up the mess.

These two engravings of the destruction of Arica, Peru, in 1868 show the dramatic association between earthquakes and tsunamis.

In many ways, with hindsight, one can identify one particular great earthquake of the not too distant past as a spur to the development of human understanding of the forces of nature, setting the enquiring human mind on a trail which led, eventually, to the modern theories of continental drift and plate tectonics. On 1 November 1755, the most violent known earthquake of modern times destroyed the city of Lisbon in Portugal and, together with an associated tsunami, killed an estimated 60,000 people while shaking a region covering 1.5 million square miles (4 million square kilometers). This was the time when science was first rising to prominence, and the great thinkers of the time were stirred by the disaster to ponder on the nature of what now seemed to be the not-quite-solid Earth beneath their feet. It was as long ago as 1760, five years after the Lisbon disaster, that English geologist John Mitchell suggested that earthquakes are caused by shifting masses of rock deep below the surface of the Earth, and thereby set succeeding generations of what came to be called 'Earth scientists' working along the right lines.

In terms of modern Earth science though, it is hard to say just how big the Lisbon quake of

1755 was. It was definitely bigger than the 1906 San Francisco quake, but there was no way of making measurements of earthquake strength in those days, and one has to go by the accounts of damage in order to judge its power. These were powerful and widespread; the shocks which killed 60,000 out of a population of 235,000 (more than a quarter) produced waves in ponds as far away as England, France, Italy, Holland and Switzerland and a slopping motion in water noted with surprise and alarm by many widespread observers. The more anecdotal material – in its way, even more impressive than the dry facts and hard statistics of modern disasters – was handed down by various men of letters, among them the Englishman Thomas Chase, whose letter home to his mother describing the quake (which he survived) was published many years later in the *Gentleman's Magazine* of February 1813.

Anxious to see what was happening when the ground began to shake, Chase climbed to the top of his house for a better view – hardly recommended procedure in an earthquake, and he was fortunate to escape with his life when the top of the house collapsed and he was thrown down amid the debris, uncon-

In the village of Gemona in northern Italy, women try to salvage what they can after the earthquake of May 1976.

scious. Recovering and struggling free from the rubble, he presented such a desperate sight that a Portuguese man who saw him, 'Started back, and crossing himself all over, cried out, as is the custom when much surprised, "Jesus, Mary, and Joseph! who are you? where do you come from?" '

Well might the passerby have asked – and well might Chase's mother have worried when reading on to find her son's description of his state: 'My right arm hung down before me motionless, like a great dead weight, the shoulder being out and the bone broken: my stockings were cut to pieces, and my legs covered with wounds, the right ancle [sic] swelled to a prodigious size, with a fountain of blood spurting upwards from it: the knee also was much bruised, my left side felt as if beat in, so that I could hardly breathe: all the left side of my face was swelled, the skin beaten off, the blood streaming from it, with a great wound above, and a small one below the eye, and several bruises on my back and head.'

This graphic description from more than two hundred years ago reveals the human impact of the statistics of disaster with which the world is all too familiar in one form or another today. Headlines screaming 'Hun-

Survivors head out of town past the Palace of the Army.

SKOPJE: THE AGONY OF '63

At the individual level, the earthquake that struck Skopje in Yugoslavia at 5.17 am on Thursday 25 July 1963 was unique, as all such events are. As people rushed out into the street in their pyjamas and nightdresses, parents scrabbled frantically in the ruins for their children. One man ran around screaming: 'They've dropped the bomb! They've dropped the bomb!' Children were found in half ruined rooms, crouching – in the words of one distraught eyewitness – 'like paralyzed sparrows in a corner.'

On a wider perspective, Skopje was an 'average' disaster. The population fled the stricken city, shrouded by a pall of brick dust and already beginning to reek of death. (One thousand had died.)

But Skopje was not to be an 'average' disaster. For some reason, it captured the attention of the West, and the international response to its plight was overwhelming. Bedding, prefabricated buildings, drugs, workers and machinery arrived in little more than a week. France, Russia, Britain, America, China – all made immediate contributions, enough to control the threat of disease and to provide adequate temporary housing before the onset of winter. By September, 40,000 workers were on their way to begin rebuilding the Macedonian capital. At the same time most of Skopje's industry started functioning again. Within a month, Skopje had received some 11 billion dinars ($18 million) from 50 countries. In addition, America offered $23 million worth of loans. Within a decade, the city had been largely restored.

dreds killed and injured in earthquake' mean little to the average reader; the tale of one victim, dragging himself from the rubble, hits home in a way that no roll-call of death possibly can.

Discovered by friends, and seemingly safe in bed with his wounds tended, Chase had still further hardships to endure – the sequel to all earthquakes which shatter great cities – fire. Almost cut off by flames, Chase was now carried to safety in the square, itself lit by the burning remains of the King's Palace.

One striking difference in this tale from those of modern disasters now appears, though. Instead of the looting and disorder which caused problems in San Francisco and elsewhere, the deeply religious populace of eighteenth century Lisbon reacted quite differently: 'The populace, it seems, were all full of the notion that it was the Judgement-day; and willing therefore to be employed in good works, they had loaded themselves with crucifixes and saints; men and woman . . . were either singing Litanies, or with a fervor of zeal stood harassing the dying with religious ceremonies.'

The rest of Chase's tale of hardship and escape makes equally gripping reading, but

Yugoslav soldiers wrestle in the heat with the masonry of a former apartment block.

NIIGATA: A PUNCH PULLED

Japan suffered its worst shock since the Tokyo disaster of 1923 at midday on 16 June 1964 when Niigata, the port and oil refinery on the northwest coast of Honshu, was shaken by a massive two-minute quake measuring 7·7 on the Richter scale (as compared to Tokyo's 8·2). Rents appeared in the street, buildings lurched crazily, bridges collapsed, oil-tanks split and ignited. Expecting the worst, thousands of the town's 290,000 inhabitants flocked to the university campus.

They escaped lightly. True, in the industrial area, oil and gas tanks burned for days, and some 10,000 people were left homeless. Yet the residential districts were remarkably unscathed. There was little danger of a holocaust like the one that devastated Tokyo: cooking fires were no longer of the open, charcoal-burning variety. And the town was (and is) built on soft alluvial ground which apparently cushioned the shock: instead of collapsing, massive buildings merely heeled over surrealistically like ships in a high sea.

A building tilts precariously on its foundations.

A line of apartment blocks heel over like ancient grave stones.

The city's buckled railway track.

Smoke billows up from the blazing oil from the 90 tanks that had established the city as one of Japan's principal oil refineries.

tells one little about earthquakes. But one reflective comment helps to complete the picture of the original disaster, the earthquake itself:

'It is universally agreed that all the mischief proceeded from the first three shocks of the earthquake, which were attended with a tumbling sort of motion, like the waves of the sea; and that it was amazing the houses resisted so long as they did. No place nor time could have been more unlucky for the miserable people. The city was full of narrow streets; the houses

A highway bridge across California's San Fernando Valley destroyed by an earthquake in 1971. The quake killed 50 people.

were strongly built and high, which, by falling filled up all the passages . . . the streets . . . were thronged with people going to or from their churches, many of whom must have been destroyed by the falling of the houses only.'

Here there are obvious modern parallels, not least in California where the tall buildings reach heights undreamed of in the eighteenth century, standing ready to topple even more destructively into the streets below. And the importance of luck, good or bad, with the timing of an earthquake is highlighted: bad luck, in Lisbon in 1755, as the thronged streets were devastated; good luck in the Los Angeles area in 1971 when a quake in the San Fernando region struck at 6 am on 9 February before the morning rush hour. Not one of the biggest quakes, but enough to do severe damage locally, it would have killed many people if it had hit a little later, since it wrecked freeway bridges and interchanges. Even this quake – which caused a mere $500 million in property damage and 50 lives – came very close to setting off that nightmare of modern disaster 'planners' – floods from fractured dams. Almost 80,000 people were evacuated from a danger zone below the dam on Lower Van Norman Lake which actually crumbled in the quake but just held while the water level was reduced to remove the danger. And this was almost a common quake – one the size of the San Fernando shake (magnitude 6.6) hits somewhere in California every

Relief workers arrive in Caldiran, the worst hit village.

Incoming helpers find just one house left standing amidst the rubble of Caldiran.

TURKEY: SUFFERING IN A WASTELAND

At 2.25 pm on Wednesday 25 November 1976 an earthquake measuring 7·6 on the Richter scale convulsed the eastern part of Turkey. In all, some 8000 people died. (The area was used to catastrophe: in 1939, 30,000 had died in a similar quake.) The worst hit village was Caldiran where only one house was left standing. Help was slow coming to this remote area on the Iranian border and workers were hampered by snow and ice. At one place, a hundred people were pulled from the rubble, only to die of exposure.

Initial relief efforts were poorly co-ordinated. A gasoline shortage hindered rescuers. Drugs were in short supply. Hundreds of bottles of freshly donated blood were left behind in Istanbul because Turkish airline authorities were unable to provide air transport for delivery – the planes were en route to Saudi Arabia loaded with Muslim pilgrims. Within days, however, a fleet of 25 US military cargo planes arrived with tents, blankets, stoves and fuel. The crisis was over – until the next time.

A girl weeps on the remains of her home.

four years or so.

The importance of timing in earthquake disaster situations is highlighted by an official US National Oceanic and Atmospheric Administration study of the likely implications of a magnitude 8.3 earthquake striking San Francisco at 2.00 pm, 4.30 pm or 2.30 am. Looking just at the figures for the 85 major hospitals in the San Francisco Bay area whose facilities are valued at over $1000 million in all: the two afternoon disasters give estimated casualties of 1300 killed and 8000 injured, with doctors and nurses as well as patients and visitors among the victims, just at a time when the rest of the city would be desperate for medical aid. The 2.30 am disaster, while still killing a likely 425 and injuring 3000 in the hospitals alone, would leave many of the medical staff on their feet and able to help others to the best of their ability.

One keeps coming back to the western seaboard of the Americas, of course, since it is there that one finds today the juxtaposition of civilization and tectonic activity which makes for disastrous earthquakes. No one is too bothered by a major quake off in the wilds somewhere. But think of the impact if – let's face it, *when* – something like the Alaskan quake of 1964 smashes through a densely populated state like California. That Alaskan disaster which is still on the American/Pacific plate boundary, has been estimated as striking with the force of a 200,000 megaton nuclear explosion, 400 times as powerful as the combined blast of all nuclear devices ever let off in man's insane war preparations over the past three decades. The wreckage of the jumbled landscape produced by this upheaval tells its own story.

Many towns were wrecked on that Good Friday in 1964, but one of the worst afflicted was the port of Seward where the calamities piled one on top of another. First the quake, then as usual, fire – but fire not just on land but in the harbor where floating oil from ruptured fuel storage tanks spread. Then, the inevitable

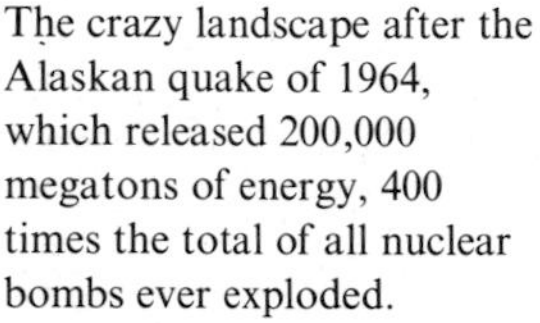

The crazy landscape after the Alaskan quake of 1964, which released 200,000 megatons of energy, 400 times the total of all nuclear bombs ever exploded.

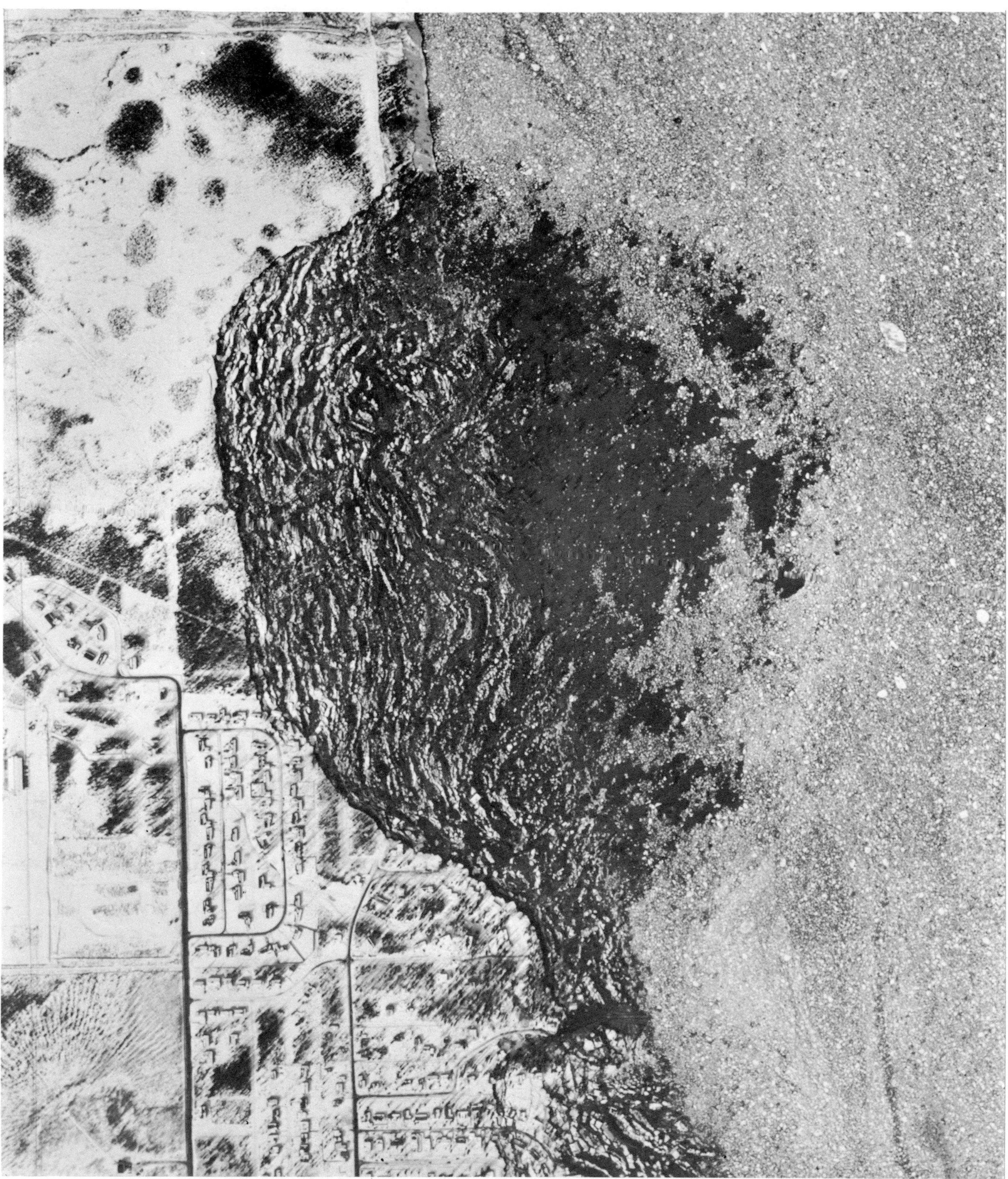

tsunami produced by earthquakes underwater hurled not just water but a wall of water covered with blazing oil inland. A flaming flood crushed homes, tossed cars about like toys, and then burnt up the remains. This was an immense tidal wave. Two thousand miles away in Crescent City, California, this same tsunami struck as a nine-foot-high tidal wave, sweeping into the city's business center and starting its own oil tank fires in a muted, but still fearsome, echo of the havoc to the north.

The roll of earthquake disaster is, if not endless, certainly long enough for familiarity to breed contempt. But some highlights re-

The effect of the quake on part of the Alaskan coastline.

Right. Guatemala City after the 4 February 1976 quake, which killed some 23,000 people and made a million homeless.

main important. Agadir, a town in Morocco, was destroyed in 1960 by an earthquake only one six-thousandth as strong as the 1906 California earthquake, but centered almost directly under the city – exact location, as well as timing, determines the extent of disaster. In the same year, severe shocks in Chile produced tsunami, set the whole of the Earth ringing like a bell, with oscillations of the whole planet being recorded at seismic stations around the globe, and shook a volcano which had been dormant since 1905 back into life. Obviously there is a need to treat Planet Earth as a whole in attempting to understand geological activity – and to study the links between those twin harbingers of disaster, earthquakes and volcanoes.

But one last lesson, for now, from one of the biggest and most recent disasters which occurred in Guatemala on 4 February 1976. There, the seismic situation had been ominously quiet since 1960 – a background of 500 small quakes a year in the 1950s had died away to a mere 250 or so tremors annually; and that means that the tension building up in the Earth's crust at this site of tectonic strain was *not* being properly released. When the tension became high enough, the crunch had to come, just as in California it is the quiet regions of the San Andreas Fault (near San Francisco and Los Angeles) that suffer occasional major disasters, while regions of gently continuous activity slip along with no big jerks.

The shock itself, on this occasion, reached 7.5 on the Richter scale, was felt from Mexico to Costa Rica, and lasted for just 30 seconds. As a result, over the next few weeks 23,000 people died, more than a million were left homeless, and about 80,000 were injured. A shift of five feet along the fault line (a strike-slip fault like the San Andreas) did the damage. It severed roads, railways and bridges, cut houses in two and changed the appearance of the

Ruins in Agadir, Morocco, after the earthquake of 29 February 1960 which completely destroyed the town.

landscape. Shattered roads were buried by landslides and villagers hit by the disaster could get help only from the all too few helicopters available.

The *National Geographic* recorded the personal impact of the catastrophe:

'In San Pedro Sacatépequez, an Indian entrepreneur named Cleto Monroy felt the earth's convulsion and, in the dark, seized two of his children. Somehow he got them out the door before the adobe walls collapsed. "I thought it was only my own house that had fallen," he said later. "When I turned on the lights of my car, I saw that the whole of San Pedro had fallen."

At the capital city's 17th-century church of Cerrito del Carmen, Father Constantino Gastino heard "a sound like an explosion – perhaps an entrance of thieves." Another man compared the sound to that of a train.

In the western part of the capital, off Avenida Elaena, a bakery fell and smashed adjoining houses, killing seven people. Luís Arturo Rodas Ortiz awoke for only an instant to the noise of crashing furniture and human screams; then the collapsing roof caught him

Two men masked against the increasing stench pick their way across the ruins of Guatemala City to check out a broken drain as a possible water supply for survivors.

and he was unconscious again.

Student Estuardo Nanne climbed out his bedroom window and held fast to the sill as the wall of his neighbor's house crashed down. "At such a moment," he said, "you feel . . . *lonely*."

To combat the risk of fire, electric power in the capital city is automatically disconnected during severe quakes. But darkness proved no handicap for a seller of lottery tickets, Edgar René Quiñones, and his wife: Both are blind. "We had been taught how to take care of ourselves," said Señor Quiñones. "My wife and I leave our clothes close by in a chair, and we had taught our children the same. Darkness was no obstacle."

Two of Guatemala's newly orphaned children.

Don Claudio Urrutia of the Guatemala National Observatory has a scientist's instant list of priorities. He was awakened by his wife. "She is my first seismograph. We had just felt P, but not yet S [for primary and secondary shock waves]. I bent over to get my shoes – and toppled onto the floor with the shock of S. Everything was dark and moving, so I felt the wall to reach the door. There I found that my wife had also fallen, so I picked her up, got her out, and said, 'Don't move.' I went back inside to get a flashlight. And then my pistol. And then my wallet, for if your house falls, you need money. And after that I went to the observatory. You know, other people run outside when an earthquake starts; scientists run *inside*. To get their instruments working again."

Don Claudio's professional priorities were matched by those of Father Constantino Gastino: "I put on my pants and then asked God for His help." In such a spirit Guatemalans began life again. One Indian remarked, "You go to sleep and awake and the world has changed."

In El Progresso the 18-year-old Alfonso Amaya Montes had heard his sister call to him in the first moments of the quake, but now he lay buried alive beneath the rubble of tiles and adobe – all that was left of the family's house. "I thought of my father and mother and wondered whether they would be saved. There was dust, dust. But I had just enough air to call. Within an hour a man with white hair managed to dig me out.

"My parents were dead. And the sister who had called me. I lost eleven relatives, and they were all buried without coffins, wrapped only in sheets. We could not have funerals. There were too many dead."

In El Progresso survivors could not even summon help: All telephone lines were ruptured, and the highway had been blocked by a hundred landslides. At dawn a messenger set out on foot for Zacapa, 37 miles (60 kilometers) away.

In the capital doctors and nurses moved hospital patients outside onto sidewalks.

"I've never seen so many fractured spines and pelvises," a surgeon reported. "Everyone was in bed when the houses fell."

"I sutured 36 spleens in 24 hours," another surgeon observed.

"We had no beds for the children the first day," a nurse told me. "They had to lie in the street. I worked just on my knees. We had only one blanket apiece for them that first cold night. Some Indian children were brought in from the highlands. They spoke only Cakchiquel, so we couldn't find out their names or home villages."'

'Traveling through the city' wrote another reporter, 'the damage you see gets worse the poorer the district is, until you come to the slums that straggle down the ravines on the edge of town – the "barrios." Here, hundreds of little landslides had taken 20 or 30 houses at a time, tumbling to the bottom of the ravine, like collapsed packs of cards. We spoke to one old man who had lived through one of those nightmares. His house had been the one on the top.'

The old problem of looting appeared, with gunfire providing a sporadic background to the efforts of survivors and rescue workers to put some kind of order back into the life of Guatemala City. The radio issued warnings of a new kind of parasite – false 'medical helpers' who gave the unsuspecting injections of morphine then made off with their victims' wallets while they were unconscious.

The facts are as numbing as that view of the dark side of human nature. Can one really understand what it means to have 58,000 houses destroyed in one city? Or to know that the rupture along the fault line could be traced for 150 miles (240 kilometers), with single cracks 33 feet (10 meters) long and four inches (10 centimeters) wide? But however 'scientific' one may try to be today, the human impact remains. And what one now calls a 'backward' country like Guatemala probably would not seem much out of the ordinary to someone like Thomas Chase, could he be miraculously transported to the twentieth century. So perhaps his account of the Lisbon disaster, among all those in this chapter, is the one to re-read and keep in mind: the picture of one man, desperately injured and struggling from the ruins of a city to meet the threat of fire.

Multiply that picture 80,000 times to get a feel for the scale of what happened to Guatemala in 1976. For, after all, the property damage is entirely secondary. What makes a disaster is its impact on human beings; now, as in 1755, the impact is all too often the same – an Old Testament catalogue of catastrophe. Humanity has a lot to learn. And the shakings of Planet Earth still have other kinds of disaster to throw at mankind in the form of the fiery associates of tectonic rumblings, the volcanoes.

Looking east along Market Street at midday on 18 April about seven hours after the quake. The fire had already destroyed acres in the center of the city and the pall of smoke rose two miles into the air.

THE 'FRISCO SHAKE

In the spring of 1906, San Francisco was booming. In this, the capital of the American West since the Gold Rush of 1849, solid buildings – the Fairmont Hotel, the new Post Office, the $6-million City Hall and countless others – symbolized the city's prosperity. Prominent San Franciscans planned newer and better developments. Though the city had been shaken a number of times and ravaged by several fires, there seemed cause for their optimism: the heart of the city was stone-built and the Fire Department was in good shape. There were only a few concerned about the hazard posed by the thousands of wooden frame buildings in which the less well to-do lived. Their fears soon proved well founded. At 5.12 am on the morning of 18 April Police Sergeant Jesse Cook, standing at the corner of Washington and Davis Streets, heard a deep rumble. He looked up and actually saw the earthquake coming. 'The whole street was undulating,' he remembered later, 'It was as if the waves of the ocean were coming toward me.' The first shock lasted 40 seconds. Buildings danced; towers toppled; church bells clanged wildly; frame houses splintered; rails, bridges and pipelines twisted 'like wet clay.' For ten seconds, there was silence, then the shake began again, for another 25 seconds. It reminded one survivor of a terrier shaking a rat. A mining engineer recalled being awakened by a sound like a gale and breaking waves, and hearing the stones of the buildings grinding together. On the steep hills, the buildings were largely unscathed, but downtown streets rose and fell 'like a hog-wallow.' Houses tumbled by the score. Men and women staggered out and stood vacantly, 'like speechless idiots' with shock. In the silence, they whispered, until called by the cries of the injured. But the quake was just the beginning of the catastrophe. Soon the city had to face the real menace: fire.

At a peak of prosperity: Looking west along Market Street, summer 1905.

An engine dashes to a blaze.

Soon smoke began to rise ominously into the sky from a score of fires – many of them amongst the blocks of flimsy wooden houses south of Market Street. The Fire Department had no alarm, but they did not need one. The horses were calmed and hitched and the engines headed for the blazes, bells clanging. Then came a terrible discovery – the water mains were broken and there was no water in the fire hydrants. Fire companies had to use the sewers and the waters of the Bay itself. By 9 am it was clear that the city was on fire and the blaze was almost certainly out of control.

Mayor Eugene Schmitz acted quickly. During the first few hours, the 1700 troops quartered locally were deployed and the mayor issued a proclamation authorizing looters to be killed.

On Russian Hill, which remained untouched, photographer Arnold Genthe, whose pictures of the catastrophe have become classics, snapped this view of the burning city. Two young girls temporarily ignore the sight to get into the picture.

The fire burned for three-and-a-half days. It caused some $400 million worth of damage. On the second day the army moved in and began to move people out of threatened houses, sometimes using force to do so. Whole sections were dynamited to created fire corridors. Nothing made much impact, and the heart of the city was gutted. Refugees crowded into Golden Gate park and Mission Park. A hundred and fifty relief stations were set up to serve hot stew and bread and on one day alone the Red Cross served 313,000 meals. Food could be had only by standing in line and waiting.

People proved remarkably disciplined. There were rumors of rioting, looting and random killings, but such stories – like the suggestion that animals and people were swallowed up by the earth – appeared in numerous newspaper reports and were widely believed, but they were almost all mythical.

An ominous notice downtown (below). A few people were shot for looting, but despite rumors to the contrary, the town remained remarkably well ordered and arrangements for the homeless – like the tent city in Golden Gate Park (bottom) – went smoothly.

The ruined observatory in Golden Gate Park, and a nearby line of refugees awaiting food (inset).

Grace Church on California Street.

Looking south from Union Street on the edge of the fire-ravaged area.

By Sunday morning the air was clear. Four hundred and ninety blocks had been destroyed. The fire had ravaged an area six times the size of that destroyed by London's Great Fire of 1666. The town seemed crumpled and diminished. Many of its great stone 'fire-proof' landmarks had vanished. Yet the spirit of the city survived largely intact. Within a week the only surviving theater was open again. Aid poured in. There was no outbreak of disease. Nobody starved. Rebuilding began immediately and nine years later San Francisco could proudly invite the world to see the results of the city's reconstruction at the Panama-Pacific International Exposition.

The shell of City Hall, shattered in the first half minute of the quake and the 1 eaten away by fire.

Mount Etna spewing out rocks and ash in May 1971.

4: ANATOMY OF THE VOLCANO

Volcanoes are perhaps the most impressive as well as among the most devastating of phenomena. Their random violence still inspires an almost religious awe. Though still all too often unpredictable, volcanoes are now well understood. This chapter reviews current knowledge about the types of volcano and the mechanisms that produce them.

The word 'volcano' makes most people picture a conical mountain with a hole or crater in the top from which flows a stream of redly glowing molten rock or lava. Such a picture is certainly a fair description of one kind of volcano, but there are many other varieties scattered around the world. Or perhaps *scattered* is not quite the right word: it seems that volcanoes like the seaside.

Very few volcanoes of any kind occur in the middle of continents; a few of a very special kind occur in the middle of oceans; most – far and away the great majority – occur around the edges of the oceans where oceanic and continental crust meet. Clearly this is no coincidence, and the distribution, like the distribution of earthquakes, can be understood in terms of continental drift and plate tectonics. (Volcanoes actually *under* the sea are a slightly different story but their occurrence still lies within the framework of plate tectonic theory.)

The most impressive chain of seaside-hugging volcanoes occurs around the world's most impressive body of water, the Pacific Ocean. Long before the ideas of plate tectonics were even beginning to be worked out, this distribution had been noted by geographers and given the dramatic name 'The Ring of Fire.' For a long time this was as mysterious as it was impressive. However, the picture of continental drift outlined in Chapter 2 can explain just why volcanoes should occur in chains around the oceans – or, at least, some of the oceans.

The key part of the theory, as far as these volcanoes are concerned, is the evidence that where spreading sea floor and massive continent meet, the sea floor can dive down under the continent where it is broken up and melted back into the material of the Earth's interior. Although that sounds straightforward enough when said quickly, such dramatic geophysical activity involves a great deal of disturbance of the Earth's crust.

A boundary where ocean crust is destroyed in this way is called, for obvious reasons, a destructive plate margin. But the destruction of oceanic crust below causes the continent above to be built up and wrinkled into great mountain ranges. The heat at the boundary where the crust is breaking up and melting forces molten rock, or magma, upwards into the continental crust, where from time to time it bursts through the overlying rock to form active volcanoes.

In some cases, the piling up of continental crust and the production of volcanoes occur down the edge of a continent, as in the case of western South America. In other cases, the 'continental' crust may be covered in shallow water between the deep trench where the

How the different types of igneous rocks are formed from magma. Welling up from the earth's interior, magma may emerge in the sea, at the coast, within other strata or in various types of eruptions. The basic constituent of magma is basalt from the earth's depths. Other types of magma include andesite and granitic magma formed by melting continental crust as it plunges back downwards at a trench.

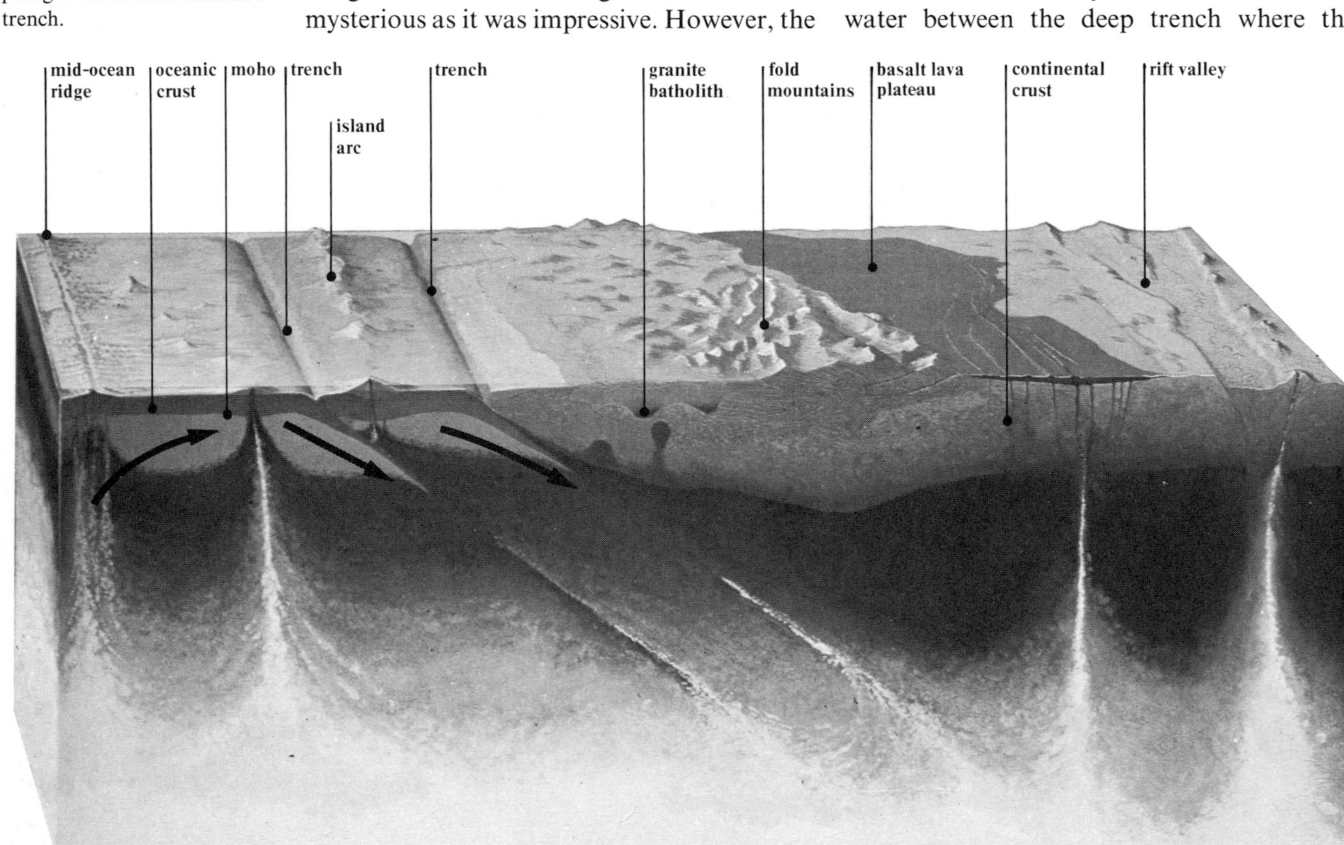

destruction occurs and the dry land which one is used to thinking of as the 'continent.' Here, the mountain building and volcanic activity produces a chain of islands, riddled with volcanoes and subject to frequent earthquakes, like the islands of Japan.

But the presence of volcanoes does not indicate that all of the Earth below the crust which makes up the shifting plates is molten. Deep down in the Earth's interior the material is certainly very hot, although geologists and geophysicists still argue about whether it can accurately be called a 'liquid.' Fortunately, our interest in the Earth, for understanding volcanoes and earthquakes, need only be skin deep. What seems to happen is that at a depth of about 45 miles (70 kilometers) (*really* only skin deep for a planet 7960 miles [12,734 kilometers] in diameter), the temperature and pressure conditions are just right to form a thin layer of molten rock which acts as a kind of lubricating oil to ease the sliding about of the plates above. It is this lubricating material, and not the deep matter from the center of the Earth, which bursts out in volcanic activity at sites of special strain.

So where else, other than at destructive margins, is the crust under great strain? Obviously one place is at the *constructive* margins, the ocean ridge systems where new oceanic crust is being created and spreading out to either side. These are, by and large, simply cracks in the thin oceanic crust where convection in the underlying material has forced magma up until it has broken through the surface. This activity, however, proceeds rather quietly by the standards of the great volcanic eruptions that trouble mankind on land. The spreading out of magma as it forms rock beneath the sea is very persistent, of course, and over the long term a dominant factor in shaping the face of the Earth. But slow, steady activity is no great trouble to mankind, and in any case there is little human activity to be affected by the persistent volcanism of the spreading ridges, with the notable exception of Iceland. Thus we can largely ignore this stress zone when we are puzzling over the effects of volcanic activity on human society today.

Occasionally, if one looks at the global distribution of volcanoes, there seem to be exceptions to the rule that volcanoes like the seaside, and the most obvious of these is in the great Rift Valley system of eastern Africa. However, on analysis these turn out to be the exceptions that prove the rule.

In eastern Africa the heat from the Earth's interior and the powerful stress induced by convection in the skin-deep layers of the surface have begun to break up not just thin oceanic crust, but the thicker crust of the continent. Africa is being torn apart, down several more or less parallel lines, and in millions of years from now the site of all this activity will have become a spreading ridge in the middle of a new ocean. In the Red Sea the same process is already well advanced, and to the geophysicist this insignificant little narrow sea is in every respect a recognizable ocean, with a spreading ridge bounded by oceanic crust. Just how far the activity will progress in Africa cannot yet be foretold, but probably one of these new spreading ridges will quieten down as the other dominates. Much the same thing happened long ago when Europe and America were split apart by tectonic activity; incipient rifts and embryonic ocean ridge-spreading systems developed in what are now the North Sea, the Irish Sea and the Atlantic Ocean, but only the latter flourished. With a slightly different pattern of events, either Ireland alone, or both Britain and Ireland, could easily have been left as offshore islands not of Europe but of North America.

Thus volcanoes occur most often at the creation or destruction of plates where the Earth's crust is under greatest stress. One last category remains, however: the 'special cases' referred to earlier in this chapter. These are associated with so-called 'hot spots' – purely local regions where a particularly active hot feature below the crust has punched a hole, or holes, in the crust above.

Hot spots can and do occur under continental or oceanic crust, but the best example is provided by the islands of the Hawaiian chain. If the crust did not move around above the hot spot, it would simply produce one enormous volcano above as it allowed magma from the lubricating layer to leak away. But as outlined earlier the crust is constantly moving, drifting over the apparently fixed position of the active hot spot below. The result is that this rising plume of hot magma punches not just one hole but a succession of holes in the crust drifting past above.

In Hawaii one sees the result as a chain of volcanic islands, far away from either the continent/ocean boundary or from the Pacific spreading ridge. The youngest island in the chain, directly over the hot spot today, is still active volcanically – Hawaii itself. The older islands, successively older as they are further

The types of eruptions: the shapes and names used to classify volcanoes here is just one of a number of accepted classifications. Any volcano and any eruption may contain a number of different features.

Hawaiian eruption.

Strombolian eruption.

Vulcanian eruption.

from Hawaii and the hot spot, are no longer active, mere remnants being carried away from the site of all the excitement.

A far cry from Iceland and the activity of spreading ridges, perhaps, but all oceanic volcanoes have one thing in common. They are made up almost entirely of basalts, the basic material of the Earth's crust which has welled up from the lubricating layer. Continental volcanoes, like those of the Andes, are made up of a much more complicated mass of material: part of the material comes from the continent scraped away and melted by the activity below; another part comes from the melting broken-up oceanic crust; and part comes from the sediments and muck of the sea floor, carried into the depths and melted along with the rest. These rocks are called *andesites*, after the archetype of the Andes themselves.

The questions '*why* volcanoes occur' and '*where* they occur' have been summarized. Now let us turn to the volcanoes themselves.

The best way to classify volcanoes is by the characteristics of the eruptions. In this system, different real volcanoes are taken as the archetypes from which whole classes get their names; the system is not ideal, since no two volcanoes are really alike, but it has the merit of being easily understood in real, physical terms.

Hawaiian volcanoes are the gentlest, by volcanic standards, and fit rather well the picture of steady but slow eruption at ocean ridges mentioned previously. The key to this calm behavior is that these volcanoes in the middle of the Pacific are driven by almost pure basalt in a very runny fluid form. This free-flowing fluid allows any trapped gases to bubble off easily, with no chance of a violent explosion because no gas gets trapped long enough for the build-up to force the volcano to blow its top. Another feature of Hawaiian volcanoes is exceptionally interesting and educational. Where a crater has been produced by the collapse of a pit at the summit of a volcano, the fluid magma can form a lake of molten material, crusted with floating slabs of solidified magma. To the delight of geophysicists, this shifting crust behaves almost exactly like the shifting crust of the whole Earth, with both destructive and constructive margins, and regions where slabs rub side by side – in the fiery mouth of the volcano, they see a working model of the Earth's tectonic activity.

Next up the scale of volcanic violence we

find the *Strombolian* eruptions, named after a volcano which forms an island between Italy and Sicily. The lava here is still basaltic, but rather thicker than that in Hawaiian volcanoes, allowing gas to build up and burst out in small explosions every few minutes, shooting lumps of half molten lava into the air. Although lava may occasionally break out from the summit crater and blow a little way downhill, Strombolian volcanoes are more noisy than dangerous, and on Stromboli itself there are two villages within a mile of the active crater. Etna, in nearby Sicily, and Mount Erebus, far away in the Antarctic, are two other examples of Strombolian volcanoes.

Roughly in the middle range of this classification scheme comes, appropriately enough, the volcano from which they all get their name: Vulcano itself. Located to the north of Sicily, Vulcano is only intermittently active but blows its top much more vigorously than either Strombolian or Hawaiian volcanoes when the fancy takes it. A *vulcanian* eruption, when it does occur, can last for months at a time blasting solid blocks of material clear of the crater, producing large quantities of ash which are spread by volcanic gases in a great plume, like smoke from a huge chimney, and perhaps building up to an outflow of lava. This is beginning to take on the familiar picture of our mental image of a volcano, although it may still be a surprise to learn that the ash can be more harmful than any flow of hot lava.

Ash can spread over a vast distance; in addition this kind of vulcanian eruption may go on for a very long time – months or even years – with great quantities of ash spread across the surrounding countryside but very little, if any, eruption of molten lava. In the famous example of the destruction of Pompeii, it was ash that did the damage; in the equally famous example of Krakatoa, volcanic dust blasted high into the atmosphere affected the weather of the whole Earth for many years.

The fourth step on the ladder of volcanic activity is named after Mt Vesuvius. *Vesuvian* eruptions produce a more persistent plume of gas and ash which forces its way higher up into the atmosphere. Just because of this increased upward blast, such volcanoes are, paradoxically, sometimes easier to live with than vulcanian volcanoes. Vesuvius itself, almost next door to the city of Naples, blows its top every thirty years or so. But when it

Vesuvian eruption.

Peléean eruption with burning cloud

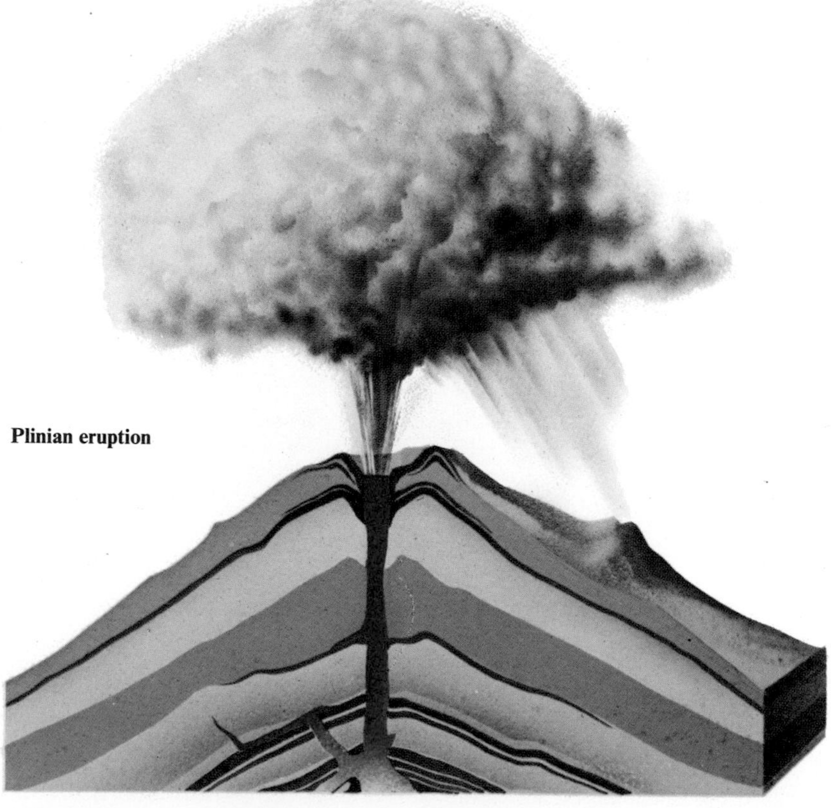

Plinian eruption

A lava bomb lying in scoria on the slopes of Mount Etna.

does the ash from the volcano is carried so high into the air – several kilometers up – that it is more decorative than harmful as it is so dispersed by the time it does reach the ground that it does no real harm.

Finally there is the last category, the real blockbuster eruptions. Vesuvius – or strictly speaking its predecessor, Mt Somma – has, indirectly, been responsible for the name given to these volcanoes, through its outburst in AD 79 which destroyed Pompeii. The eruption was the cause of the death of Pliny the Elder, who either ventured too close in his eagerness to observe the events and was overcome by fumes or, more probably, suffered a heart attack through over-exertion and excitement in trying to study the volcano from close quarters. The account of his death, recorded by his nephew Pliny the Younger, has come down to us and given the name *Plinian* to the biggest volcanic explosions of all. In a Plinian eruption, the amount of ejected material is almost mind-boggling. Pompeii, five miles (eight kilometers) away from the center of activity in AD 79, was covered by three yards (three meters) of volcanic debris and pumice. It has been estimated that in that eruption Vesuvius spewed out one cubic mile (three cubic kilometers) of material in 48 hours. This is the kind of volcanic eruption that can shatter its own crater to produce a depression miles wide, or may destroy volcanic islands entirely as in the case of Krakatoa in 1883. Fortunately for mankind though, such dramatic outbursts are as rare as they are powerful.

Thus two features of volcanoes are of key importance in determining the destructiveness of an eruption: the stickiness of the magma flowing out through this break in the Earth's crust, and the amount of ash and other debris blasted out in the process. The gas which bubbles out from the lava – easily from fluid lava, erratically and explosively from the thicker variety – is mainly water vapor, probably the last thing the uninitiated would expect to be associated with the fiery activity of a volcano. But this water escaping from the mouths of volcanoes is of crucial significance to planet Earth. Together with the gases that make up our present atmosphere, the water of the oceans has all come from volcanic outgassing long ago in the history of the Earth.

This seems hard to credit today with only about 500 active volcanoes scattered around the surface of the Earth, and probably no more than 25 of these erupting actively in any one year. But, of course, in its early history the Earth was a much more violently active planet, and the great forces and frictional heating involved in dramatic events such as the capture of our Moon must have stirred up a veritable cauldron of volcanic activity about 3500 million years ago. Even now, the relatively quiet continuing volcanic activity can still disturb the balance of the atmosphere and thereby play a part in molding the changing climate of the Earth, as discussed later. But it is the solid material that is produced by volcanism that matters today; the gases are

A forest destroyed by a *nuée ardente* or burning cloud, from Arenal, Costa Rica, in 1968. The volcano is concealed by fumes in the background.

only important because they power the explosions that blast the solid material clear.

For dramatic impact, and an equally dramatic name, it is hard to beat the 'bombs' of solid material blasted out during volcanic eruptions of the more extravagent kind. The name is entirely appropriate for fragmants of solid or semi-solid lava hurled into the air as spinning, rotating lumps which seem to hang lazily above the observer until they hit the ground and stick where they lie, or burst into fragments, or go rapidly bounding and hurtling down hill at an incredible speed. Do not be misled by the term 'fragments.' The ejected material can easily form man-sized (or larger) lumps thrown for hundreds of yards around the center of volcanic activity – hardly surprising when the energies involved rank well up alongside the most destructive explosions produced by man. Although it is the most extreme example known, the eruption of Tambora in 1815 provides the yardstick; it was estimated at 16,000 megatons, or 800,000 times as powerful as the atomic explosion that destroyed Hiroshima! Bombs weighing tons hurled for hundreds of yards may be rare but are certainly possible products of volcanic eruptions.

The dramatic naming of the bombs extends down to the descriptive labels given to the different kinds and shapes of material ejected. Sticky lava hurled into the air forms a solid crust which cracks open on hitting the ground, giving a so-called *breadcrust* bomb; ribbons of lava which twist and solidify as they fly through the air are *ribbon* bombs; round lumps, logically enough, are called *spherical* bombs; long, spindly ejecta are dubbed *fusiform* bombs; and material which splatters into a pat on landing is called, for obvious reasons, a *cow-dung* bomb.

Rather less imaginative names are given to the other kinds of ejected solid material. All the bits and pieces of solid material shot out by volcanoes are called *tephra; bombs* are the largest pieces; medium sized pebbles and grit are called *lapilli*; the smaller fragments are simply called ash and, smallest of all, dust. Although the bombs are the most dramatic form of tephra to any observer, it is the other extreme, the ash, that makes the effects of volcanic eruptions most disruptive and widespread.

Apart from the truly global effects on weather which will be discussed later, the smaller fragments of material can form a kind of avalanche of material sweeping out from the volcano to engulf anything in its path. These hot avalanches may simply be composed of lava, reaching out over a sloping mountainside until it breaks off under the tug of gravity and hurtles down into the valley just like any solid avalanche, even a snow avalanche. This type of avalanche is bad enough for those in the valley below, but much worse is the kind of 'avalanche' known as a *nuée ardente*, a violently active hot avalanche in which tephra is suspended in a wall of advancing gas. Supported and swept along in this way, the ash can cover a very great distance in

The molten magma which feeds volcanoes is a combination of lava and volcanic ash. Before eruption, magma is under a pressure equal to the weight of overlying rocks. As it rises, gas separates as bubbles and the magma starts to froth. In a slow eruption, the gas separates before it reaches the surface, but if the rise is rapid, gas and rock are blasted up together as in the Hekla, Iceland, eruption shown at far right.

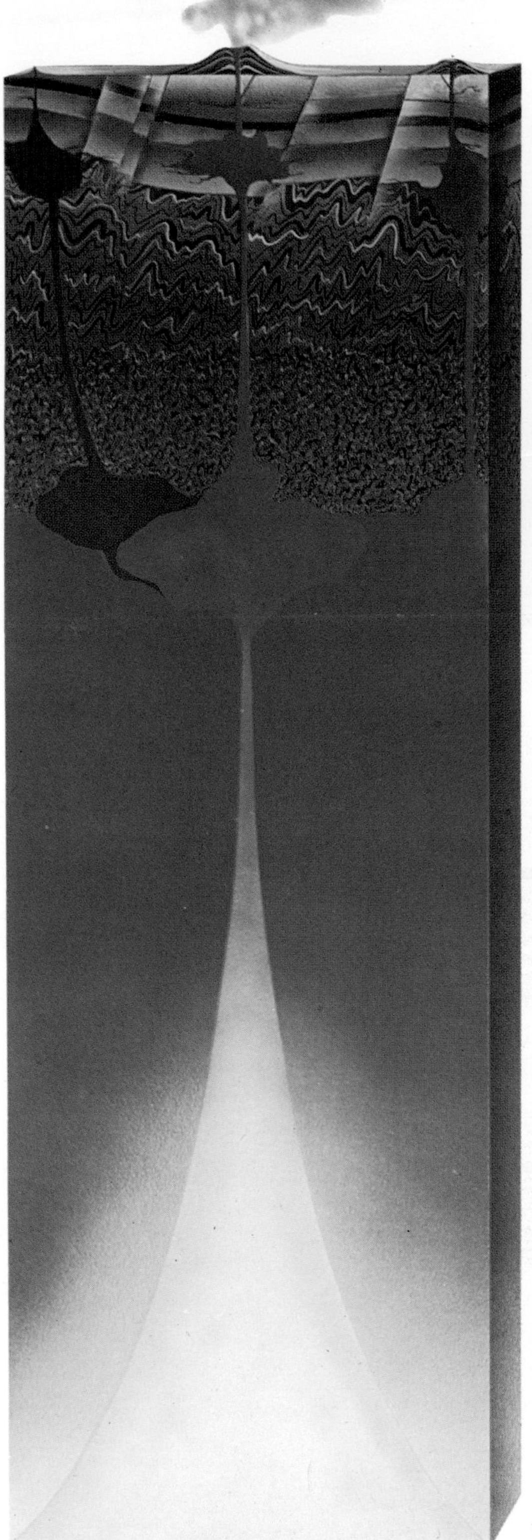

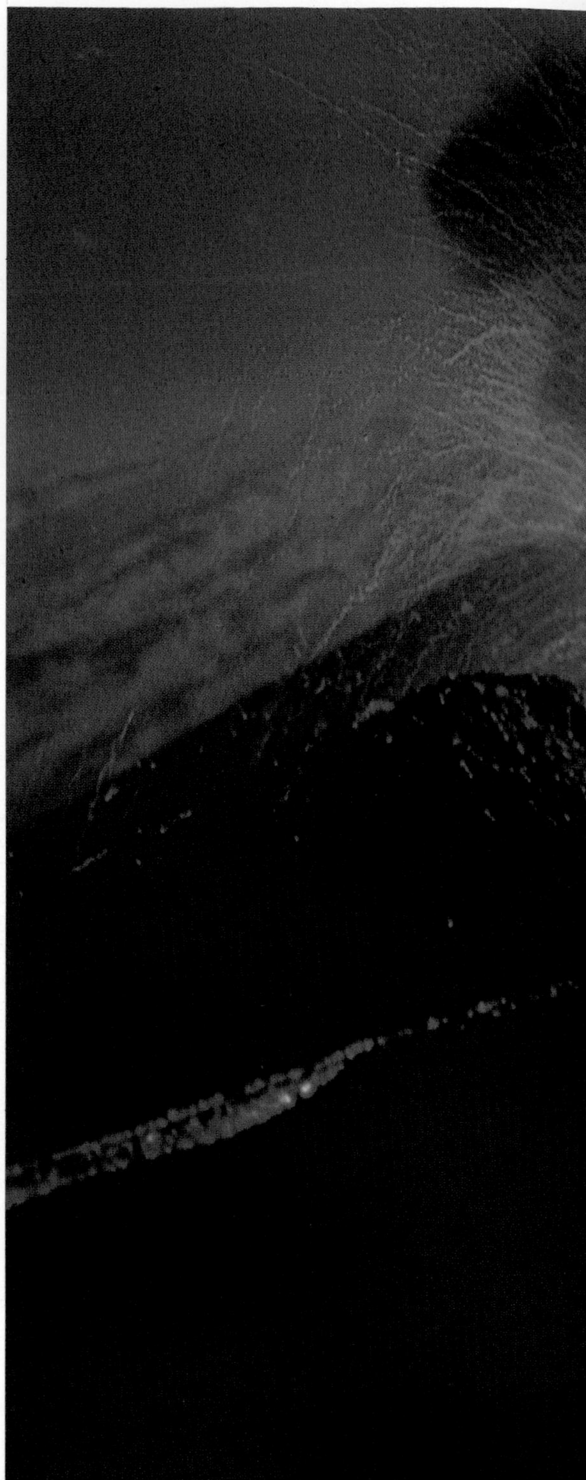

a very short time.

The classic example of this kind of avalanche is the eruption of Mount Pelée in Martinique in 1902; indeed, this eruption was so dramatic, and its effects on the nearby town of St Pierre so disastrous, that many Earth scientists use the term 'Peléean eruption' as a special category to describe eruptions dominated by the outpouring of nuees ardentes. However, since this kind of activity is usually just one feature of the overall activity of a Vesuvian or Plinian eruption, this definition of a sub-category all of its own does seem to be a little hair-splitting.

Indeed, the 1902 eruption of Mt Pelée is itself best described as Vulcanian, with irregular bursts of activity, loud explosions and showers of ash including several other nuées ardentes before the fateful day, 8 May, which ensured its place in history books forever.

The phenomenon which produces this kind of hot avalanche is familiar today in another even more grim context, as the 'base surge' which rolls away from the site of a nuclear explosion at ground level. And the destruction caused by a nuée ardente which hits an inhabited region can only be compared with the destruction caused by a nuclear explosion.

Even in bare outline the story of the destruction of St Pierre reads more like the horrors of war than any natural disaster. The preliminary activity of the volcano, from 23 April 1902 onwards, had itself produced large quantities of ash and sufficient gas that reports tell of animals dropping dead in the streets of the city, some three miles (five kilometers) away. With explosions in the volcano's crater building up, flowing hot avalanches of ash and rivers of boiling mud produced several deaths in regions around the volcano during the three days from 5–7 May; then, at about 8.00 am on 8 May the biggest explosion of the eruption blasted away a chunk of the crater wall, sending hot gas and ash out sideways instead of straight up, as is typical of Vulcanian eruptions.

This blast of gas and ash, the nuée ardente which killed a city, spread rapidly down the valley of the River Blanche towards the sea, while the base surge spread on either side, sweeping across the city and its 30,000 inhabitants. Most of the devastation in the city was caused by the gas, hot enough to melt glass and metal, killing everyone in its path and leaving behind a smoldering ruin where the city had been, covered by a thin layer of

A tunnel where lava once flowed out, Tenerife.

A slow-moving lava flow on Arenal, Costa Rica.

Lava boulders on Arenal.

ash. The bulk of the ash that had swept down the mountainside coated the river valley with thick deposits of volcanic debris.

Within two minutes the disaster was over, and 30,000 people had died in the hot blast which was traveling at a speed estimated at 95 miles (150 kilometers) per hour. The temperatures – still about 800° to 1000°C (1800°F) even five miles (eight kilometers) away from the initial blast – had twisted glass and metal into bizarre 'modern sculpture' shapes, and set fire to the wooden decks of ships in the harbor, some of which were capsized by the strength of the hot wind. The few survivors of the disaster, who provided eyewitness accounts of the events described here, were almost entirely crew members of these ships, although two inhabitants of the city did survive.

Although fortunately rare, this kind of Peléean, or 'sideways Vulcanian,' eruption has proved to be by no means unique. Several other instances of nuée ardente activity have been observed – some in Martinique – since 1902, and the big surprise, perhaps, is that the phenomenon had not been officially recognized until the destruction of St Pierre. The ash laid down by nuées ardentes characteristically forms a fine, widely dispersed layer which can, with hindsight, be recognized in geological strata from much older eruptions – as, indeed, can the whole spectrum of volcanic products.

Moving down the scale from the extreme of glowing clouds composed chiefly of hot gas with ash and dust suspended in them, there is the kind of volcanic material which is filled with a froth of gas bubbles but has just proved itself strong enough to set solid before the bubbles can burst the material apart; these 'semi-solid' lumps can join up with one another to form a 'rock cloud'. This material is *pumice*, solid rock so full of bubbles that it is light enough to float on water. Less dramatic than a nuée ardente? Perhaps – but it was a layer of pumice that buried Pompeii in AD 79, so it can hardly be dismissed as an innocuous volcanic product.

Whatever its source, these ashes and solid debris from volcanic eruptions must eventually fall to the ground where they are squeezed down by other geological layers and pressed into a solid given the general name, *tuff*. Tuffs which are actually welded by heat, not just the pressure of everyday geological processes, are dubbed *ignimbrites*, and these layers have a similar appearance to solidified layers of lava – the last general kind of volcanic product (leaving gases aside for the present).

Paradoxically, the hot flowing lava that provides the dramatic pictures and is synonymous with volcanic activity is now seen as the least dangerous product, and the least significant in everyday terms, although on geological time-scales it has achieved the rather important feat of building up the entire solid crust of the Earth as it is known. Flowing lava varies tremendously in form, from thin, runny streams to thick, cooling material moving sluggishly forward like a slow-motion avalanche; as already discussed, the composition of the lava also varies, depending on just where the volcano is sited, and what products have gone into the melting pot through the workings of the plate tectonic 'machine' that is the Earth's crust. The result is an extensive variety of solidified remains, many of them forming dramatic views where they still lie on the surface, but the details of which are of more interest to the geologist than to the general reader.

Fortunately, once again the geologist has given appropriate descriptive names to the end products, such as *blocky* lava, *ropy* lava and a form, characteristic of lava produced underwater, *pillow* lava. The names alone are sufficient to indicate the general characteristics to the casual reader.

Before moving on to look at the more dramatic and, in the short-term, more significant effects of disastrous explosive eruptions, one should spare a thought for the patient workings of quieter volcanoes, like those of Hawaii, where great volumes of lava, but little in the way of dramatic outbursts of gas and ash, have spilled out over the ages.

Such volcanoes are, in fact, the biggest. They characteristically form a very shallow cone, or dome, which is supposed to resemble a shield lying on its side, giving them the name *shield* volcanoes. The lava they produce comes not just from a central vent but also from eruptions on the flanks through cracks and fissures opening out like the arms of a fan radially around the central peak. Mauna Loa in Hawaii reaches a peak of 13,675 feet (4171 meters) above the sea floor, the high point in a 'shield' stretching across more than a hundred miles (160 kilometers) at its base at the bottom of the ocean. At least one known shield volcano is even more impressive; the Olympus Mons on Mars stands 18 miles (29 kilometers) above the surrounding plain, and

Balls of lava below El Teide, Tenerife.

Ropy basalt lava in Iceland.

Bands of ash and pumice at 13,000 feet, El Misti, Peru.

THE SHAPE OF MAGMA

Magma intrudes into the crust largely by sheer force, shouldering apart the rocks. Solid rock is also disintegrated by magma into blocks (*xenoliths*), most of which are melted or chemically digested by the magma. Some magmas, especially those formed at great depths, rise through the crust by a process of *fluidization*, whereby the magma drills its way up as a turbulent mixture of hot gas and solid fragments. If it finds an outlet, it may either run out as lava or be blasted out in volcanic ash. This may form a rock known as *ignimbrite*.

Intrusions of magma cool underground (below) to form igneous rocks which are seen at the Earth's surface only if erosion removes the overlying rock (right). Intrusions are commonly revealed in prominent landmarks exemplified by the *plug*, or infilled conduit of an old volcano. *Dykes* are steep, sheet-like intrusions. *Sills* are sheets which follow the bedding of strata and are relatively flat-lying; less fluid magma may form the rarer, blister-like variant known as a *laccolith*. Large, deep intrusions or *magma-chambers* act as reservoirs which feed volcanoes. Deep, sill-like masses make up huge complex intrusions in some continental areas. Deep-seated masses of granitic magma may rise as huge blobs, like oil in water, to solidify as *plutons* within a few miles of the surface.

Right: Ignimbrite exposed by erosion at 13,000 feet in Bolivia.

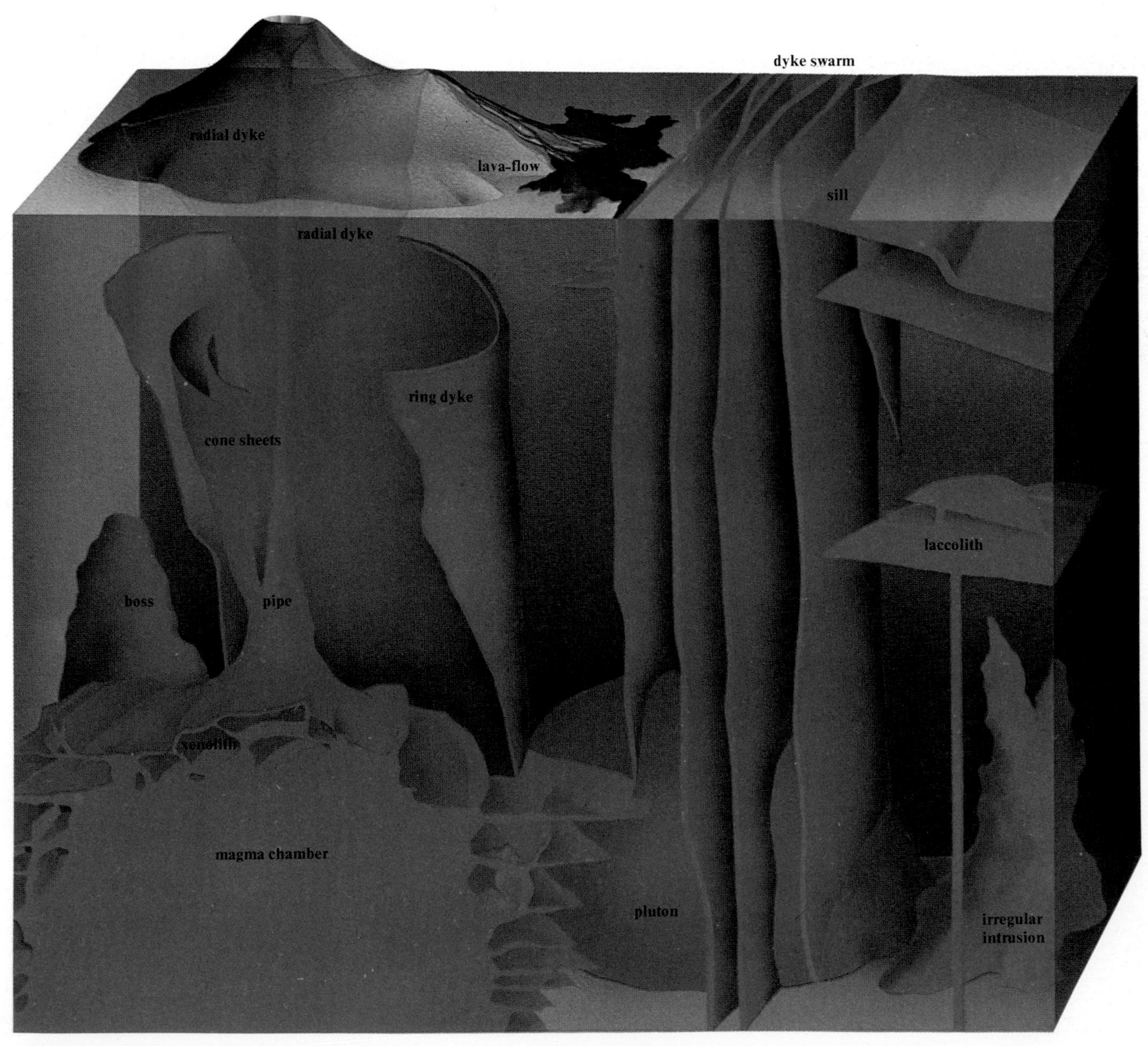

Right. Stromboli in explosive eruption in 1971.

contains as much material as all of the shield volcanoes of the Hawaiian system put together. In the history of a planet, and on the scale of a whole Solar System, shield volcanoes are by far the most dramatic. But in a human lifetime and over the scale of a city, it is the explosive eruptions that matter.

Most people, living far from active volcanoes, see them as dramatic phenomenon of only local significance. In fact, volcanoes have world-wide effects on atmosphere and climate. One of the best ways to develop a picture of the significance of volcanic processes in shaping the atmosphere and climate of a planet is gained by looking at our near neighbor, Mars.

Mars today is a dry planet with a very thin atmosphere, inhospitable and possibly devoid of life. Yet Mars and Earth started out in very similar fashion in their young days, a couple or three thousand million years ago, and the differences seen today are largely due to the slightly smaller mass of Mars, which has a weaker gravitational pull than the Earth and has therefore allowed most of its valuable atmospheric blanket to escape into space.

It was the advent of a the dramatically successful Mariner 9 and Viking space-probes in the 1970s that brought Earth-based astronomers their first close-up pictures of planet Mars, and indicated the great changes that planet has experienced. The battered Martian surface today resembles in some ways that of the Moon, with many craters of all sizes marking the impacts of large or small meteorites with the Martian surface. But the same pictures show another, strikingly unexpected picture of the planet – dried up river beds, deserts marked by the flow of past floodwaters, and a great deal of other evidence that fresh water once flowed on the surface of Mars. They also show great volcanoes, including the Olympus Mons; by putting all these pieces together a coherent picture of the climatic history of Mars emerges.

The key discovery came from counting the number of impact craters that cut across the lines of the old river beds on Mars. Clearly the craters were formed after the rivers stopped flowing, and since it is known roughly how many new craters form each year – or, rather, in each million years – from comparison with craters of the Moon and other bodies in the Solar System, it is possible to work out roughly how long it has been since the rivers ran dry. The incredible result of the calculations of the cratering statistics is that the river beds are, at the very least, hundreds of millions of years old. The days when Mars was a warm, wet planet with a thick atmosphere are long past – but the way in which it ever got such an atmosphere at all echoes the way in which Earth's atmosphere developed.

Both planets formed from material orbiting the Sun, gathered together under the tug of gravity to form battered planets with no atmosphere, repeatedly gathering up more debris in the form of meteorite impacts, and becoming cratered like the Moon. The atmospheres of the planets developed initially from the heating of the rocks in their newly formed interiors, squeezed by pressure from above or molten by the blasting impact of meteorites. Volcanoes and outgassing from the rocks in less violent form would produce the same gases that are released by volcanoes today – atmospheres rich in methane and ammonia, well laced with water vapor which, as the planets cooled, condensed to form water.

From here on, the history of the two planets deviated. On Mars the photochemical reactions caused by the sunlight would liberate light gases from the atmosphere, since a breakdown of ammonia, say, to liberate hydrogen would let the light hydrogen escape from the weak Martian gravity. On Earth the lighter gases liberated in this way were more easily retained. On both planets oxygen produced when sunlight broke up water molecules in the primary atmosphere must have

The largest volcano known – Olympus Mons on Mars – about 18 miles (29 kilometers) high. The crater alone is 45 miles (70 kilometers) across.

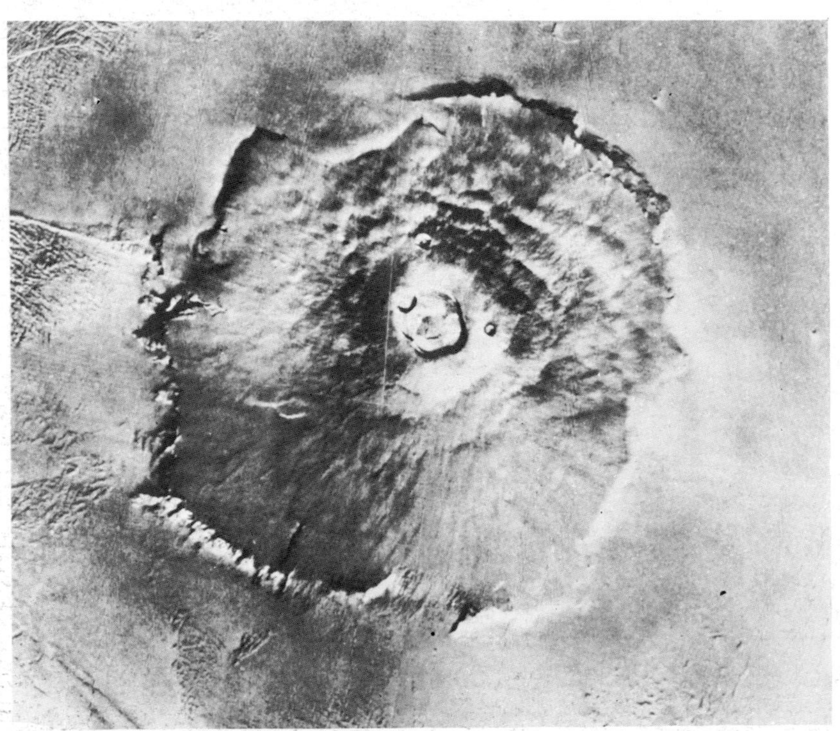

THE NIGHTMARE OF 'EN MOD'

The prospect of future eruptions to shake up our earth-based civilization might seem quite enough to worry about. But now, for the first time in history, a new factor is acting to disturb the equilibrium of our shaking Earth – the activities of mankind. The prospect of inadvertently triggering some disastrous change in the natural balance of our environment is grim enough; far worse is the possibility, now seriously entertained, that geophysical forces might be unleashed deliberately in acts of war known as 'hostile environmental modification,' or 'en mod.'

By and large, the triggering of earthquakes and/or tsunamis is not a practicable means of waging war today; anyone crazy enough to wage war on a grand scale could do more harm to the opposition by conventional use of nuclear weaponry. But volcanoes, at least in certain special cases, provide a much simpler way to trigger disaster, whether accidentally or by design.

Because active volcanoes are already sites at which the hot lava from deeper layers in the Earth's crust is brought to the surface, it is easy – in principle – to trigger a volcano into life. One might imagine tossing a nuclear bomb into a quiescent crater to set things going. But this is a bit pointless if the intention is to cause harm to the major industrialized cities of say Britain, the US or USSR, since not may of these are located on the slopes of active volcanoes. But if an explosion on the scale of Krakatoa could be triggered, the extremely widespread effects might be seen to work to the advantage of certain states. Cooling at high latitudes, severe winters and so on would hit the developed northern nations much more severely than those of the Third World.

At a time when world resources are limited and unevenly distributed, when the recession in the developed world is leading to an even greater reluctance to share the cake with the poorer relations, and when large population increases stretch the existing world food supply and distribution system to the utmost, the possibility of some kind of nuclear blackmail of the rich nations by the poor is now discussed openly as a serious possibility by some politicians and futurologists.

The key to this prospect lies in the innocent sounding realm of the study of fuel coolant interactions (FCIs), which can produce violent explosions of vapor with no chemical interactions involved. FCIs are a potential hazard in industries where hot and cold liquids may come into contact, such as the steel industry where molten steel mixes with water. In that case the steel is the 'fuel' and water the 'coolant' but these terms are only relative. Another industry where care has to be taken to avoid violent FCI explosions is the nuclear power industry, where in some reactors liquid sodium is used as a 'coolant' and the 'fuel' which might trigger the explosion would be molten uranium oxide.

Although the details of such interactions are not thoroughly understood it is clear that by coming into contact with a vast source of heat from the 'fuel' the coolant can, under some conditions, be turned to vapor very quickly, expanding explosively and throwing the hot droplets of fuel over a wide area. Hardly a prospect to be relished in a steel factory or nuclear power station – but what if the fuel is molten lava pouring from a volcano into the sea?

Clearly this kind of activity does not usually – or even occasionally – produce an FCI explosion. Except on extremely rare occasions, lava pushing into the sea does not *mix* with water, and the two liquids are separated by a clear-cut boundary. Of course the water at the boundary is heated and may boil into vapor, but without any violent mixing of lava and steam to produce shattering explosive power. The key to the explosive power of the two fluids – and perhaps to the next Krakatoa – is that a large area of the two fluids must be

combined with carbon from the rocks to form carbon dioxide. But while on Mars even this escaped, by and large on Earth the carbon dioxide blanket remained, ready to be used by the early plants and converted into the oxygen-rich atmosphere on which the existence of all animals, including man, depends.

From here on, one must leave the story of the development of Mars to go its seemingly barren way, and look only at planet Earth. But even here the volcanoes had by no means finished their role in the development of atmosphere and climate which are so important for mankind.

First, though, a word of warning. The reasons why the climate changes are very poorly understood even today, although some of the factors which *contribute* to such changes can definitely be picked out from the confusion. Because most scientists work in fairly narrow, specialized disciplines they tend to discount the broader picture. For example, when an astronomer finds a flicker in the Sun's activity that affects the weather he tends to brought into rapid contact. A theory developed at the Culham research laboratory in Britain indicates what probably happens next. As a vapor bubble forms in the cool liquid initially, the vast bulk of neighboring cold liquid causes it to condense and re-collapse, leaving a gap into which coolant collapses, producing a jet which blasts into the fuelant. When this jet penetrates the hot liquid, then conditions are ideal for explosive vaporization. The new bubble of exploding coolant is surrounded by fuel and rather than collapsing expands outwards, spattering the hot fuel among the remaining coolant like the spray from a depth charge, producing the complete mixing which triggers the final explosion.

All this is still hypothetical. But in 1973 an experiment which might have proved the theory right once and for all, while incidentally destroying Iceland, was halted only in the nick of time. The experiment, planned jointly by the Icelandic Government, the Coast Guard Service and the US Navy, was proposed when the flow of lava from the Heimaey (Iceland) eruption threatened to block off a vital harbor – and far from planning to test the FCI explosion process the intention of the planners was simply to set off a small charge of explosive, breaching the lava crust and encouraging the flow of lava away from the critical harbor entrance.

It was only at the last minute that Dr S A Colgate and Dr Thorbjörn Sigurgeirsson, in charge of the planned attempt at lava diversion, realized the potential dangers. As they reported in the scientific journal *Nature* a few months later, the problem with their modest efforts at volcano control was that even a small explosion, punching a hole in the relatively cool crust of solidifying material that usually forms a barrier between the hot molten lava and the cold sea water, would provide ideal conditions for an FCI explosion, by suddenly mixing the two fluids.

How much energy might be released? The experts calculated, when the dangers were realized, that they would be dealing with the equivalent of a hefty nuclear bomb. When one cubic centimeter of lava cools down from a typical temperature of 1100°C (2012°F) to the temperature of boiling water (100°C or 212°F) the energy liberated is nearly 3000 Joules. Even if some of this energy is dissipated without all its force going into the resulting explosion, it seems that only five grams of lava involved in such violent cooling provide an explosive potential equivalent to one gram of TNT – and there are many tons of lava ready and waiting to interact with the cooling water in such a situation. The trigger effect of a mere 22 lb (ten kg) of explosive set off in front of the lava flowing into the sea off Heimaey harbor could, according to Colgate and Sigurgeirsson, have resulted in an explosion equivalent to a four megaton bomb – the equivalent of four *million* tons of TNT.

If anything, this estimate is on the conservative side. For once such a large explosion occurred, the rocky structure of the whole island would be torn asunder, allowing sea water to pour in on to the fiery lava at the heart of the volcano and setting off as a second stage in the explosion an even more violent blast. Tens – even hundreds – of millions of tons of lava, even hotter than 1100°C (2012°F), would be involved in the resulting 'great-grandaddy' of all FCI explosions. Is it then any longer a mystery how the Krakatoa eruption managed, starting from just this situation of an eruption on a volcanic island, to produce a blast estimated by some authorities as equivalent to 200 megatons of TNT? Even the more conservative volcanologists, setting a figure of 'merely' 50 megatons to the size of the Krakatoa eruption, would still be left with a power awesomely greater than any desperate poor states might otherwise be able to exploit and a temptation which, given the world situation outlined above, must make this kind of interaction of serious interest in the world today. Enough volcanic islands exist around the world for the deliberate triggering of the 'next Krakatoa' to be physically possible.

assume that this is the main driving force behind climatic change.

In the same way, an oceanographer may believe that changes in ocean currents drive the Ice Ages; a glaciologist may point to changes in the Antarctic ice cover; and a volcanologist will get excited about the effects of dust in the atmosphere. All these effects probably contribute to changes in climate on Earth, and volcanoes are among the most important. But it would be a rash person indeed who claimed that *all* of the great changes in terrestrial climate and the broad sweep of Ice Ages in the past, could be accounted for by the effects of volcanic dust *alone*.

There are several ways in which volcanic dust, blasted high into the atmosphere, can cool the Earth and disturb climate. But one should remember that other factors too are constantly at work, and that even Professor Hubert Lamb, Director of the Climatic Research Unit of the University of East Anglia, and probably the greatest Western authority

An explosion crater, long extinct, at Malha in Sudan.

The ancient cone of Nevado de Sajama in the Bolivian Andes.

on the effects of volcanoes and climate, has said that although volcanic activity does have effects of the right kind to produce widespread cooling, the occurrence of large-scale volcanic activity is too infrequent to explain the known pattern of past Ice Ages.

Even so, the effects of volcanoes on the climate are dramatic enough. After large outbursts of volcanic activity, with several eruptions in a few years, the measured amount of solar heat reaching the surface of the Earth can fall by as much as 10 to 20 percent. It is just as if the dust blasted up into the atmosphere acts as a sunshield or umbrella, reflecting away into space part of the heat from the Sun that would otherwise reach the ground. Krakatoa alone produced a measurable dip in the curve showing the amount of heat received from the Sun under cloudless skies; another dip in the curve in the early 1900s and up to about 1920 has been explained as caused by the eruptions of Mount Pelée in particular and of other volcanoes in the same decades. Up until quite recently, though, the rest of the twentieth century has been fairly quiet in volcanic terms, and one must look back in history to take the story further.

Leaving aside the ultimate climatic catas-

A perfect example of a newly formed miniature scoria cone in the Atacama Desert of Chile.

The strato-volcano Cotopaxi (19,812 feet, 6039 meters) in Ecuador.

trophe, a full-blown ice age, and looking mainly at the past thousand years or so – long enough, by any human standards – the influence of volcanoes can still be clearly seen. Professor Lamb has developed a 'Dust Veil Index,' calibrated from the recent great volcanoes, which provides a guide to the veiling effect over the past centuries. This index ties in well with climatic changes and, indeed, with changes in everyday life brought about by those climatic shifts.

Great volcanic eruptions around the globe in 1883, 1888, 1902 and 1912 provide the key data, which show their influence through falls in solar heat reaching observatories in North and South America, Europe, India and Egypt of more than 20 percent in some months, and with smaller but persistent effects lasting for two or three years. If this seems surprising – in particular, if it seems odd that local, short-lived volcanic eruptions can have long-lasting, global impact – one need only look at what happens to the dust blasted out from the fiery mouths of erupting volcanoes.

Note that here one is not concerned with the pumice, ash or nuées ardentes that cause so much havoc in the immediate vicinity of the eruption, but with the much finer dust that is carried aloft to produce pretty sunsets. The rising column of smoke, dust and debris – as typical of volcanic activity as any flow of molten lava – can be described, for convenience, in three categories which indicate the extent of the resulting 'sphere of influence.' First, the top of the dust plume may remain within the lowest layer of the atmosphere, the troposphere, in which the *weather* (not climate) is shaped. Rising no more than nine miles (15 kilometers) high, this dust will be quickly washed away by rainfall and return to Earth. At the other extreme, a very fine haze of dust and water vapor may sometimes be carried to extreme heights, above 30 miles (50 kilometers), where the convection of the upper atmosphere (mesosphere) will carry it higher still to help in forming the very thin ultra-high clouds known as ultra-cirrus or noctilucent clouds, at an altitude of about 50 miles (80 kilometers). But these fine particles play no great part in shielding us from the Sun's heat.

The most important category of volcanic dust, in climatic terms, is the middle range of material which reaches a height of 12–15 miles (20–27 kilometers), in the atmospheric layer called the stratosphere. Here, are found reasonably large particles which have been carried above the weather layer of the troposphere and can spread around the globe as a volcanic sunshield, with effects lasting for months or years before the dust slowly disperses and drifts back down to the troposphere to be washed back to the ground.

'Reasonably large,' in this case, is simply a relative term, for even these stratospheric particles are no more than one or two micrometers in diameter (a micrometer is a millionth of a meter, or a thousandth of a millimeter). Taking a one micrometer particle as typical, its lifetime in the stratosphere before falling back into the rainy troposphere can be calculated quite straightforwardly; from 25 miles (40 kilometers), such a particle has a 'lifetime' of two to three years, and starting out from 12.5 miles (20 kilometers) altitude it would take between six and 18 months for the particle to float down into the troposphere. Smaller particles persist for even longer.

Millions upon millions of such particles are ejected in large volcanic eruptions. Even in an unspectacular year like 1970, it has been estimated that 25 million tons of particles less than five micrometers in diameter are produced by volcanic activity. With such particles spreading around the world like the dust from Krakatoa, it is hardly surprising that the effects should be felt through the influence on solar radiation. The pretty sunsets themselves are produced by the scattering of the Sun's light from these particles, and since heat is, like light, electromagnetic radiation, it too must be scattered. Small wonder that researchers like Professor Lamb have found that many of the coldest and wettest summers in Europe, America and Japan are associated with years of volcanic activity – more graphically, with 'volcanic dust years.'

Particularly good examples of this link between volcanoes and climate are provided by the years 1912, 1903, 1879, the 1840s in general, 1816, the 1760s, 1725 and 1695, taking England alone, and it is intriguing to look through the history books and records of diarists such as John Evelyn with a new insight once the years of special interest have been pointed out.

Of course, the volcanic dust years must first be identified, and while this is straightforward in some places (for example, Iceland and Japan over the past few hundred years) there is also a great need for expert skill in interpreting secondhand records, ranging from accounts of remarkable sunsets to analysis of the fine layers of volcanic ash deposited in sediments around the world. Even with no human records at all, evidence is available, as in the case of the bristlecone pine trees of California. There, the long-lived trees high in the mountains have remained undisturbed by man, adding a growth ring to their girth each year. With modern precision techniques, the experts not only can count these rings in a sample of wood to find which ring was growing in a particular year, but can even identify the damage caused by unseasonable frosts within an individual growth ring. This, together with the growing evidence on volcanic dust years from a variety of proxy records, shows unambiguously that rare cases of frosts occurred between August and September near the upper treeline of these Californian pines precisely in those years of the past millenium when dust veils from volcanoes were obscuring the atmosphere.

Moving from the details of specific years and individual eruptions to the broad pattern of the past 300 years or so, the overall influence of volcanoes, indicated by Professor Lamb's Dust Veil Index, can be related to the broader pattern of climate and the affairs of mankind.

The seventeenth century itself was a time of vicious weather by the today's standards. Rivers such as the Thames froze solid often in winter; late spring frosts (and early autumn frosts) were the rule rather than the exception; and farmers were hit by a succession of extreme weather conditions, including both droughts and floods. Such a pattern of extremely variable weather is now known to go hand in hand with slightly cooler conditions over the globe, and the seventeenth century marked the deepest trough (in England) of the period from the fourteenth to the nineteenth centuries that has come to be known as the 'Little Ice Age.'

A slight recovery towards more clement conditions after the early 1700s was followed by a shorter relapse back towards cold and extreme variability early in the nineteenth century, but in the twentieth century – at least, up to the 1950s – the climate improved to become warmer and more even-tempered in the Northern Hemisphere than in any other 50-year period since AD 1000. Many of these features – not least the warming of the twentieth century – can be seen to 'coincide' with the presence or absence of volcanic activity; one can have a high degree of confidence in Lamb's Dust Veil Index.

The weather changes also tie in with other influences, of course, and it is clear that volcanoes play only a part in the complex interaction of events that determine our climate. The most accurate explanation of climatic fluctuations since the seventeenth century has been made by two US scientists, Drs Stephen Schneider and Clifford Mass, who combined the Dust Veil Index effect with changes in solar heat attributed to flickers in the Sun itself. However it is evident that the volcanic dust effect has to be included, even if it does not dominate.

By and large, the world has been lucky in having few large eruptions in the past 50 years. But in 1976 the island of La Soufrière threatened to blow its top in an explosion to rival the 1888 blast of Krakatoa or the Mt Pelée eruption early in this century. It did not happen, but it is only a matter of time before something similar really does happen – and then *everyone* will feel the consequences.

The world's agricultural machine is today balanced on a knife edge, barely able to produce and distribute enough food for the present global population. Judging by the evidence of Krakatoa, just one truly major volcanic blast could cool the world by as much as 1.5°C (2.7°F) over a period of two to three years, with an associated shortening of the growing season by frosts in spring and autumn. That would hit the whole of the world as no previous disaster of its kind. Be warned: the next 'Krakatoa' – and it could happen any day – will mean a whole lot more than a succession of colorful sunsets!

Can scientists say anything sensible about the association of volcanoes and climate on an even broader scale, up to and including the ice ages? Now one really is moving into the study of the 'proxy' records pure and simple: the layers of volcanic remains left in the rocks and the scars on the rocks produced by moving glaciers, combine with other evidence to tell the tale, but one cannot be sure which way round the tale is to be told. One thing clearly emerges; the occurrence of the Little Ice Age coincided with a 400-year-long wave of unusually high global volcanic activity that ended (or paused?) early in this century – further confirmation of the significance of the picture painted above. But further back in time the picture is more confused. One thing is clear: times of increased glaciation, including full ice ages, are very often times of increased volcanic activity. But which came first? It's the old 'chicken and egg' puzzle. Do the volcanoes cause the ice age, or does the ice age cause increased volcanic activity?

Absurd as it may sound at first, the latter prospect seems the most likely. What happens, some scientists have suggested, is that as ice builds up in great quantities on the northern continents, pressure builds up correspondingly on the rocks below. Something has to give, and when it does the result is almost certain to be a spate of volcanic eruptions with magma forced up through the rocks like toothpaste squeezed out of a tube.

That is far from being the end of the story, however. Something other than volcanic dust may have started the spread of the ice – a change in the ocean currents? a flicker in the solar furnace? – but whatever the root cause there is now a wave of increased volcanism producing its share of dust and veiling the Earth. The result may well be, if enough volcanoes are stimulated into life, a further spread of the ice, a hastening of the development of the Ice Age, and another wave of volcanic activity. So it goes on – and with such a complex system of interactions, it is no wonder that no climatologist would stand, hand on heart, and say '*this* is the cause of ice ages.'

The eruption of 1822

VESUVIUS: A VOLCANO THROUGH THE AGES

Vesuvius, towering over the Bay of Naples in southern Italy, could lay claim to be the best known volcano in the world: hemmed by cities for some 2000 years, its record of activity is unrivaled. Its site is that of a vastly greater prehistoric crater, part of which is marked by a lofty semi-circular ridge called Monte Somma. At the beginning of the Christian era, no eruptions had been known and the mountain seemed perfectly safe. Its sides were heavily populated and richly cultivated with fertile vineyards. In AD 63 there were signs that Vesuvius' long period of quiescence was coming to an end: Seneca recorded an earthquake in that year. In AD 79 the mountain exploded and buried the nearby cities of Pompeii, Stabiae and Herculaneum, an event well recorded by Pliny the Younger. Since then, there have been several dozen eruptions. By the 17th century, however, the eruptions had taken on a certain regularity. Quiescent periods were followed by active periods, ending with an explosion that apparently closed the volcano's throat for several years, until lava found its way around the plug. With most eruptions, the shape and size of the mountain changed by several hundred feet as did the shape of the crater, a process particularly well-documented by the previously unpublished series of paintings shown in this picture feature which portray Vesuvius from the late 18th to the mid-19th centuries. Discovered in the Oxford Museum in 1978, they originally formed lecture illustrations owned by Reverend William Buckland, Oxford's first Professor of Geology and later Dean of St Pauls.

Vesuvius's last great eruption was in 1944; the inhabitants of Naples may well wonder uneasily when they are due for another outburst of lava and ashes.

The excavated ruins of Pompeii

The Younger Pliny's account of the AD 79 eruptions which buried Pompeii has become a classic. He was staying with his uncle and adopted father, Pliny the Elder, at Misenum on the northern tip of the Bay of Naples when the eruption began: 'On the ninth of the calends of September,' Pliny wrote later to Tacitus, 'about the seventh hour, my mother informed [my uncle] that a cloud appeared of unusual size and shape. . . . The cloud (the spectators could not distinguish at a distance from what mountain it arose, but it was afterwards found to be Vesuvius) advanced in height; nor can I give you a more just representation of it than the form of a pine-tree, for springing up in a direct line, like a tall trunk, the branches were widely distended . . . It sometimes appeared bright, and sometimes black, or spotted, according to the quantities of earth and ashes mixed with it. This was a surprising circumstance, and it deserved, in the opinion of that learned man, to be inquired into more exactly . . .'

A victim of the Pompeii disaster embalmed in rocks and ash.

Pliny the Elder then made his way across the Bay to rescue a friend at Stabiae without any apparent sign of nervousness. He and his friend's family decided to flee. 'They covered their heads with pillows bound with napkins: this was their only defense against the shower of stones. And now, when it was day everywhere else, they were surrounded with darkness, blacker and more dismal than night, which however was sometimes dispersed by several flashes and eruptions from the mountain.' Soon thereafter the Elder Pliny was overcome, 'stifled, as I imagine, by the sulphur and grossness of the air. . . .

[In Misenum] it was now six o'clock in the morning, yet there was but a faint and glimmering light. The house shook violently; and though we were in an open court, yet, as it was very narrow and built almost all round, we were certainly in great danger. We then thought it expedient to leave the town: the people, distracted with fears, followed us, and (such is the nature of fear which embraces, as most prudential, any other dictate in preference to its own) they pressed upon us and drove us forward. When we were out of reach of the buildings we stopped; our astonishment was great, nor were our apprehensions less, for the carriages which we had ordered out of the town were so violently shaken from side to side, although upon plain ground, that they could not be kept in their places even when propped by heavy stones. The sea, too, seemed to be forced back upon itself, repelled as it were by the strong concussions of the earth. It is certain that the shore was greatly widened, and many sea-animals were left upon the strand.

On the land side a dark and horrible cloud, charged with combustible matter, suddenly broke and shot forth a long trail of fire, in the nature of lightning, but in larger flashes . . . Not long after, the cloud descending covered the whole bay, and we could no longer see the island of Capreæ or the promontory of Misenum . . .

The ashes now fell upon us, however, in not great quantities. I looked back. A thick dark vapor just behind us rolled along the ground like a torrent, and followed us. I then said, "Let us turn out of this road, whilst we can see our way, lest the people who crowd after us trample us to death." We had scarce considered what was to be done, when we were surrounded with darkness, not like the darkness of a cloudy night or when the moon disappears, but such as is in a close room when all light is excluded. You might then have heard the shrieks of women, the moans of infants, and the outcries of men. Some were calling for their parents, some for their children, some for their wives: their voices only made them known to each other. Some bewailed their own fate; others the fate of their relations. There were some who, even from a fear of death, prayed to die. Many paid their adorations to the gods; but the greater number were of the opinion that the gods no longer existed, and that this night was the final and eternal period of the world. . . .

A little gleam of light now appeared. It was not daylight, but a forewarning of the approach of some fiery vapor – which, however, discharged itself at a distance from us. Darkness immediately succeeded. Then ashes poured down upon us in large quantities, and heavy, which obliged us frequently to rise and brush them off, otherwise we had been smothered or pressed to death by their weight . . .

At last this darkness, which now was drawn into the thinness of a cloud or of smoke, went off; true day appeared. The sun shone forth, but pale, as at the time of an eclipse. All objects that offered themselves to our sight (which was yet so weak that we could scarce bear the return of light) were changed, and covered with ashes as thick as snow.'

The forum of Pompeii as it is today, showing Vesuvius in the background, five miles away.

The eruption of 1794: This produced 15 mouths and a river of lava up to 40 feet thick which partially destroyed the town of Torre del Greco.

1822: In this eruption the top of the cone fell in, lowering the mountain by 800 feet.

1845: One of the countless minor eruptions.

1845: The minor cone inside the crater during a quiescent period.

The eruption of May 1872.

Italians pose on top of a lava flow that destroyed Boscotrecase in April 1906.

In 1888 a staid English threesome pose sitting on the lava flow of 1858.

A local points out a fumarole in 1898.

Vesuvius today, slumbering peacefully.

A wartime labor gang clears away the ashes after the 1944 eruption.

:THE
ERUPTIONS

of the volcanoes that have had a particularly powerful impact on mankind.

Spectators watch the dramatic – but mild – displays provided by broad, shield-like Kilauea in Hawaii.

If the name San Francisco has become synonymous with earthquake disaster, then to an even greater extent to most people the name Krakatoa conjures up just one image – a violently explosive volcanic eruption. As an archetype of the violence pent up in volcanic sites, Krakatoa could hardly be bettered. First, it occurred at a site which is now seen as fitting perfectly into the new understanding of global tectonic activity, an island near Java on the western side of the notorious 'Ring of Fire' which rims what is now seen as the great Pacific Plate.

Next, the scale of the eruption seems to have been dramatically increased, in terms of explosive power, by the way in which sea water could rush in and mix with the molten lava. The Krakatoa disaster of 1883 also highlights the way in which volcanoes can spread their side-effects far and wide, in the form of a destructive 'tidal wave' and the more insidious effects mentioned in the last chapter of dust blasted into the high atmosphere to produce a measurable cooling of the entire globe over a period of several years as it blocks out heat from the Sun.

Perhaps the greatest difference between volcanoes and earthquakes as far as local residents are concerned, is the way in which the former give precursor rumblings before they let loose – at least on many occasions. In the case of earthquakes, as we have seen, it is

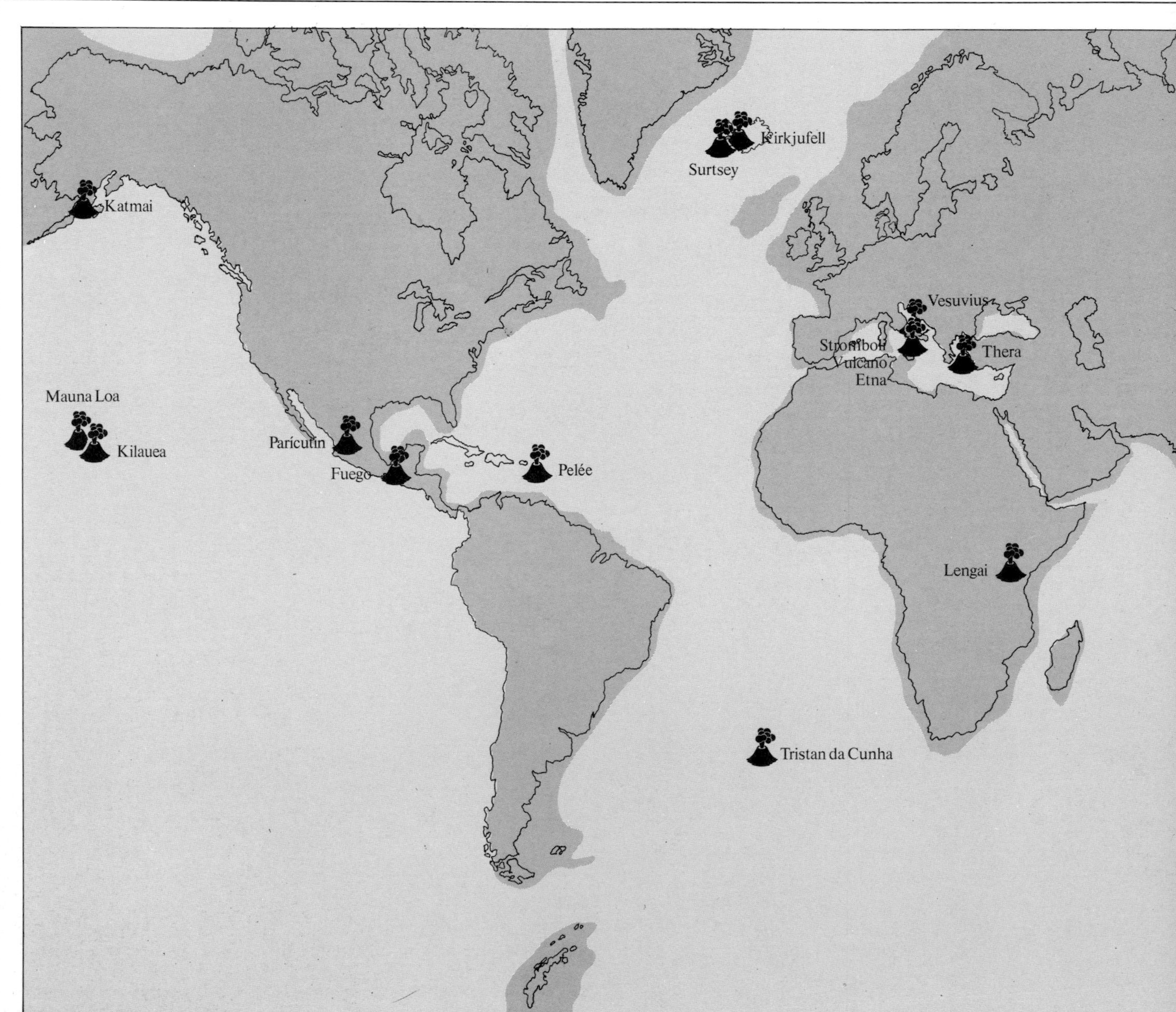

ominous *quietness* that can be the most worrying intimation of disaster. But volcanoes generally let one know they mean business, although unfortunately its not easy to tell how *much* business is intended.

Krakatoa, for example, after being quiet for about 200 years, coughed into life on 20 May 1883 (interestingly, just three years after a minor earthquake in the region, itself probably related to the volcano's activity) with an eruption powerful enough to produce a noise like distant artillery fire and a sprinkling of volcanic ash over two towns on the island of Java, more than 100 miles (160 kilometers) away. Over the next few days, ships passing through the busy Strait between Sumatra and Java – a 15-mile (24-kilometer) wide gateway from the Indian Ocean to the South China Sea, and a key shipping route – reported a great column of dust and smoke rising above Krakatoa, and pumice floating on the surface of the ocean.

By 26 May it seemed safe for a party to visit the site of the activity; it found Krakatoa and nearby islands covered in white ash, and a continuing state of volcanic activity in which clouds of pumice were blasted up to great heights from time to time. All this impressive activity was coming from a vent on the flank of the mountain which itself rose 2674 feet (812 meters) above sea level and was taking place just about 400 feet (120 meters) from the

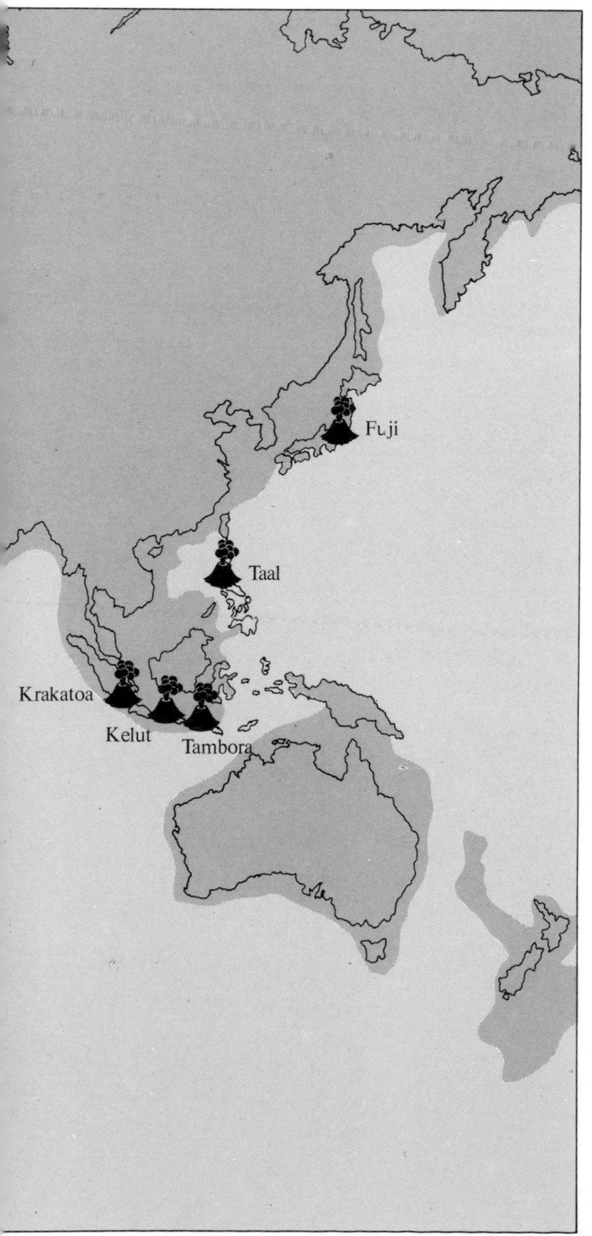

VOLCANOES: THE TOP TWENTY

Some of the most dramatic – and destructive – eruptions. The volcanoes concerned have erupted on other occasions as well.

Date	Volcano	Number of victims
c. 1450 BC	Thera	Unknown thousands
AD 79	Vesuvius	Unknown thousands
1815	Tambora, Indonesia	66,000
1883	Krakatoa, Indonesia	96,000
1888	Vulcano, Italy	—
1890	Fuji, Japan	—
1902	Mt Pelée, W. Indies	29,000
1911	Taal, Philippines	1,335
1912	Katmai, Alaska	—
1919	Kelut, Java	5,110
1930	Stromboli, Italy	—
1940	Mauna Loa, Hawaii	—
1943	Paricutin, Mexico	—
1955	(Ol Doinyo) Lengai, Kenya	—
1963	Tristan Da Cunha	260 refugees
1964	Surtsey, Iceland	—
1971	Kirkjufell (Heimaey), Iceland	—
1971	Kilauea, Hawaii	–
1971	Etna, Sicily	—
1971	Fuego, Guatemala	—

The jagged coastline of present day Thera – the rim of a huge underwater crater.

THERA: THE ORIGIN OF ATLANTIS?

The legend of Atlantis has long fascinated the west. The story of an island empire that sank into the sea in a single dire catastrophe was recorded by Plato. The modern theory of plate tectonics forbids the idea that a large island could actually have sunk in the Atlantic. Scientists now believe the civilization was Crete, the island Thera (also spelled Thira, and now known as Santorini), and that the explosion, Krakatoa-like, happened about 1450 BC. The explosion must have been truly enormous. An island 10 or 12 miles (16–18 kilometers) across was turned in an instant from a 5000 foot (1500 meters) peak into a lagoon. Such an explosion – four or five times that of Krakatoa – could have sent a huge ash fall and a massive tsunami across the 70 miles to Crete, as well as burying its own major city, Akrotiri, now being unearthed.

Pots excavated from the Minoan ruins of Thera.

The ruins of Akrotiri, unearthed beneath a protecting roof.

shore; this proximity of fire and water-line may well have been responsible for later events.

Through July and into August the volcano continued to rumble, and a further visit on 11 August showed three active craters and at least 11 active cracks in the rock. This now began to be a cause for concern, not only because of the danger to the 36,000 or so inhabitants of the immediate region of the Strait, but also because of the hazard to shipping. Even the worst of these growing fears, however, was completely dwarfed by what actually happened on 26 and 27 August.

By the afternoon of the 26th, the violence of the eruption had increased so much that instead of sounding like distant gunfire in Batavia, 100 miles away, it began to rattle windows and shake pictures hanging on the walls of the houses. Already, the violence and the rain of hot ash had overwhelmed the 36,000 local inhabitants. But the explosions which placed the name Krakatoa firmly in our folk memory were yet to come.

It seems very likely that the great explosions on the afternoon of the 26th breached the rock between at least one of the active craters and the sea, allowing a disastrous mixing of two opposites – the worst possible combination of the four ancient 'elements' of air, earth, fire and water. What happened must be supposition, since no one in the Strait survived to tell the tale. One theory, which was accepted for many years, was that sea water entering the active vents cooled the surface lava, setting it into a solid plug behind which pressure built up until a great explosion uncorked the hole again; this now looks like a rather unlikely pattern of events, and as outlined in the previous chapter modern investigations of similar situations are beginning to reveal how mixtures of 'fuel' (lava) and 'coolant' (water) can, in appropriate circumstances, produce an explosion to rank with the biggest H-bombs in any nuclear arsenal on Earth today.

Whatever the details, however, the effects were decisive. Four explosions occurred on 27 August, at 5.30 am, 6.44 am, 10.02 pm and 10.52 pm. The third explosion was by far the biggest, judging by the evidence of distant observers. And, of course, only distant observers survived to report their observations.

Some of those observers were very distant – the explosions were heard more than 2000 miles (3200 kilometers) away in Australia, and more than 3000 miles (4800 kilometers) away in Mauritius. From Batavia, however, came survivors close enough to the scene to paint a graphic picture of the disaster.

On the 26th, a Sunday, the general opinion among the alarmed citizens was that another volcano had begun to erupt, much closer to

Before-and-after views of Krakatoa, the island that blew up in 1883 in the world's largest recorded explosion. Thirty-six thousand died in the wave it caused and the explosion was recorded 3000 miles (5000 kilometers) away as 'the roar of heavy guns.'

hand. After all, Krakatoa was 100 miles (160 kilometers) away, and it just did not seem reasonable to blame the window rattling on such a distant scapegoat. The shakings and rumblings raised the alarm still higher when, at about 2 am, the gas supply to much of the city was disrupted and the lights went out, and when the Monday morning dawned it was cold and dull with temperature at an unprecedented low, by local standards, of 65°F (17°C). At first, people set off to begin the working week; but then they began to be overwhelmed by a rain of fine ash from the increasingly black sky. This continued for hours – and one witness, the British Chaplain in Batavia, Reverend Philip Neale, recorded how the terrible prospect affected different citizens.

Many of the local inhabitants were Mohammedans, and Reverend Neale recorded their instinctive reaction as one of accepting the will of Allah and settling down to await their fate. On the other hand, the Chinese showed more of a belief that 'while there's life there's hope,' and set off as quickly as possible for safety – after gathering up their valuables, that is. Twenty-five thousand Chinese attempting to evacuate Batavia at once did nothing to ease matters, however, and into this chaos came the usual result of tectonic activity in coastal regions, a tidal wave.

A view of the eruption in its early stages.

HAWAII: THE MOLTEN CORE

On the southeastern shore of Hawaii – the youngest island in the archipelago – is its youngest, most active volcano, Kilauea. The volcano stands over a 'hot-spot' in the ocean floor from which magma pours continuously, carrying the islands above with it as it forms new continental crust. One day, Kilauea will be choked off and replaced.

Meanwhile, its great fire-pit of molten lava forms what is arguably the world's most dramatic volcanic sight. Occasionally the vast pot overflows, spilling rivers of molten rock down the slope at speeds of up to 35 mph for many miles.

Left. Lava explodes out of Kilauea, setting fire to surrounding forests.

Below: Lava pours over the edge of Kilauea's crater.

A volcano 'desolation trail' in Hawaii's Volcanoes National Park.

Kilauea is a public spectacle. Hawaiians flock by bus and car to watch the mountain's latest activities, for the mountain is seldom deadly. Other volcanoes – like Vesuvius or Krakatoa – contain sticky lava that can form a solid plug, trapping gas under immense pressure until its is blasted out in stupendous explosions. In Kilauea, however, with its runny lava, gas escapes easily and seldom explodes.

When lava overflows, it may pour through a forest, hardening around the trunks of trees, burning the wood and leaving the skeletal remains behind in a deathly landscape of rock. But this charred no-man's land of volcanic warfare does not remain devastated for long. If undisturbed by new lava, plants and trees soon recolonize the lost land.

Three years after an eruption, greenery begins to return.

Batavia itself suffered relatively little from the tsunamis, since the city lay two miles (three kilometers) from the shore, to which it was connected by a canal. Even so, the streets of the capital were flooded to a depth of several feet, and the surrounding countryside inundated. The worst was now over, and even the skies began to clear. But when people ventured out by boat to the coastal region proper they met a scene of complete devastation. Whole villages were destroyed, and communications disrupted by broken telegraph lines. When the news did come in, it told of a tidal wave 100 feet (30 meters) high, not just villages but whole towns destroyed, and a death toll of more than 50,000 from these 'side-effects' of the eruption, to be added to the 36,000 dead in the immediate vicinity of Krakatoa.

But the roll of death is not, for once, the most impressive feature of the disaster. On this occasion, the very geography of that vital Strait linking two oceans was altered. Small islands had appeared where none were known before, and just about two-thirds of the island of Krakatoa had gone completely, destroyed in a 200 megaton explosion, and collapsed into a new crater well below sea level. From more than 2000 feet (600 meters) above sea level, the center of the island collapsed into a crater more than 1000 feet (300 meters) below sea level – but it is still an active volcanic site, as was shown in 1952 when a new conical island poked its smoking head above the surface, and was dubbed Anak Krakatoa, meaning 'child of Krakatoa.' Will this new volcanic peak build up to another great explosion? If so, however well the inhabitants are evacuated from the immediate neighborhood the next time around, one thing is certain – little can be done about the dust blasted up into the stratosphere.

In 1883 according to some estimates, five cubic miles (20 cubic kilometers) of debris reached the upper atmosphere, producing colored sunsets and tinted skies around the world for many months. In the 1880s temperature averages over the whole northern hemisphere fell by about $\frac{1}{2}$°C (1°F) – caused, many climatologists believe, by the dust from

Krakatoa in 1933. A submarine crater just off the island of Krakatoa blasts rock and water 4000 feet (1200 meters) into the air. This picture was taken after a local observation station detected volcanic activity and a small plane, lent by the Dutch government, flew out to the eruption.

Krakatoa today (above) and its newborn volcanic offspring, Anak Krakatoa, 'the child of Krakatoa' (below).

the massive explosion acting as a shield against the heat of the sun. Even now, a century after Krakatoa, the world would be hard pressed to do anything about that kind of overall impact on the environment. But still, not all volcanoes at watery sites explode with such violence, and perhaps one can gain some comfort from more recent events in the region near Iceland, where a new volcanic island has emerged from the sea *without* blowing its top disastrously.

On 14 November 1963 the crew of a fishing vessel off the Westman Islands south of Iceland spotted a great upheaval in the sea which could mean only one thing – volcanic activity along part of the underwater extension of the active volcanic system which slices Iceland in two. Even in the early 1960s it was appreciated that Iceland formed the above-water part of a much more extensive region of volcanic activity in the Atlantic Ocean. But that was before the establishment of the new theory of global tectonics, and nobody then appreciated the true significance of this zone of activity – what is now known as a spreading ridge literally forcing the Atlantic wider apart as new oceanic crust is created.

So the birth of Surtsey has even more significance with hindsight than it did for the excited geologists who rushed to the sc

SURTSEY: ISLAND BORN IN FIRE

On 14 November 1963 an Icelandic fishing vessel reported an explosion near the volcanic Westman Islands, a few miles off Iceland. The following night a narrow black ridge broke the surface of the sea. Accompanied by an impressive array of pyrotechnics – a column of smoke seven miles high, explosions, steam, rain of pumice stone – a new island, Surtsey, was being born. In April 1964 a regular lava eruption began, ensuring that Surtsey would remain as a solid new addition to the map. Within a few months, scientists had found the first seeds, stalks and even a live moth. The new island was alive, well, and, for a time at least, peaceful.

Clouds of steam and ash mark the birth of Surtsey.

Surtsey's first plant life.

Inside the crater, now quiet.

1963. The whole of Iceland seems to have been created from upwelling material at the mid-Atlantic ridge, and the island itself is still growing. Surtsey represents the birth of Iceland in miniature; if the new material of Iceland is eventually welded on in tectonic collisions to other land masses, then it may well be that Iceland itself will show how the very continents have grown from more humble beginnings over hundreds of millions of years by the addition of new material.

By continental standards the Surtsey eruption was tiny. Yet by human standards even a tiny eruption is awesome to behold. First, even to break surface the sub-sea eruption had to build up a cone of loose, ashy material to a height of 425 feet (130 meters) above the sea floor. Then, a column of smoke and debris from the smoking cinder of island rose as much as 50,000 feet (15,400 meters) in the air – clearly visible from Reykjavik, 75 miles (120 kilometers) away – while the island itself grew as volcanic debris poured up and out. By 16 November the height of the volcano above sea level reached 130 feet (40 meters), and it extended in a narrow ridge some 1800 feet (550 meters) long. But then came the crucial development which made the island a more or less permanent feature, and not just a passing phenomenon.

First, the island took on a much more circular shape as ash, pumice and debris continued to rain down from a vent rising now more than 500 feet (150 meters) above the sea. Stretching more than a mile (1.5 kilometers) in diameter by March 1964 – about four months after the initial outburst – Surtsey was about half as big as Central Park in New York. But ash and pumice alone cannot make a stable land mass; flows of lava are needed to weld the whole thing together and create a more permanent feature. On 4 April 1964 this last piece of the construction of Surtsey fell into place when lava began to flow from the central vent. The eruption was of the classical Hawaiian type – the beginnings of a process which would ultimately build up a shield volcano. This provided another landmark for the geologists: it was the first time anyone had ever observed the birth of a shield volcano, although Iceland itself contains many broad domes produced by this kind of activity in the past. Given enough time – millions of years – Surtsey may eventually grow to meet the mainland of Iceland, a real, permanent addition to the landmass of the Earth.

In spite of this dependence on volcanic and other tectonic activity however, as the example of Krakatoa illustrated, these fires remain a menace to anyone who happens to be nearby at the wrong time. The potential for disaster is also borne out by the events following the Mt Pelée eruption in 1902. The eruption itself, of course, was described in the preceding chapter as an archetypal example of the violence of this kind of eruption. But what remains to be told, bringing out the full horror of the situation far more effectively than the dry statistics, is the tale of the two survivors from the destroyed city of St Pierre.

Some books even today still report the story of the prisoner in an underground cell in the city jail as that of the 'only survivor'; presumably, in a macabre way, it is neater and more romantic to have just one man left to tell the tale of disaster. But the truth is that there were two survivors, and indeed both their stories were published within a year of the events that took place in May 1902.

The prisoner's tale first, since it has already become the 'stuff' of legend. Auguste Ciparis was his name, and his story was taken down within days of the eruption while he recovered from his wounds in a temporary hospital set up by the priest of the neighboring Morne Rouge district. The reports tell us that although still showing the effects of 'frightful burns which his back and legs had received' Ciparis was 'sufficiently composed to give a clear and dispassionate account of his sufferings.'

On 8 May Ciparis was waiting for his breakfast when suddenly it grew dark and hot air began to flow into his cell, gently but persistently, carrying with it a burden of ash, through the grill in the door. Immediately burned, he cried for help but received none – indeed, there was no one to answer his cries. To add to the terror of the situation, there was no noise in the cell, just complete darkness and the insistent burning of hot air and ash, which worked under the shirt and trousers of the victim to burn his flesh without setting fire to his clothes. For three days Ciparis lay, badly burned, in his dark cell, without food, although his water supply was unaffected (a fact that almost certainly saved his life). On the Sunday after the disaster (which happened on a Thursday), search parties scouring the desolate remains of the city came within earshot and heard his cries. Breaking through the fine ash piled over the site, they released the half-dead prisoner and took him to the priest for attention to his burns.

The second story is, in a sense, less dramatic in that the survivor was just lucky, it seems. On the other hand, his story is reported verbatim in the pages of the Bulletin of the *Société Astronomique de France* for August 1902 – and that makes the tale of 28-year-old shoemaker Léon Compere-Leandre more valuable in many ways than the second-hand reports of the events affecting Auguste Ciparis:

'On the 8th of May, about eight o'clock of the morning, I was seated on the door-step of my house, which was in the southeastern part of the city, and on the Trace road (the road from Saint Pierre to Fort-de-France which abuts, almost in the center of the city, upon the street Petit-Versailles). All of a sudden I felt a terrible wind blowing, the earth began to tremble, and the sky suddenly became dark. I turned to go into the house, made with great difficulty the three or four steps that separated me from my room, and felt my arms and legs burning, also my body. I dropped upon a table. At this moment four others sought refuge in my room, crying and writhing with pain, although their garments showed no sign of having been touched by flame. At the end of ten minutes, one of these, the young Delavaud girl, aged about ten years, fell dead; the others left. I then got up and went into another room, where I found the father Delavaud, still clothed and lying on the bed, dead. He was purple and inflated, but the clothing was intact. I went out, and found in the court two corpses interlocked: they were the bodies of the two young men who had before been with me in the room. Reentering the house, I came upon two other bodies, of two men who had been in the garden when I returned to my house at the beginning of the catastrophe. Crazed and almost overcome, I threw myself upon a bed, inert and awaiting death. My senses returned to me in perhaps an hour, when I beheld the roof burning. With sufficient strength left, my legs bleeding and covered with burns, I ran to Fonds-Saint-Denis, six kilometers [3.7 miles] from Saint Pierre. With the exception of the persons of whom I have spoken, I heard no human cries; I experienced no degree of suffocation, and it was only air that was lacking to me. But it was burning. There were neither ashes nor mud. The entire city was aflame.'

It hardly seems worth trying to follow such a graphic description with further personal details of the horrors of volcanic eruptions. But perhaps one can draw back a little from the details of personal narrative and look at the broad impact of two other eruptions: Tristan da Cunha in 1962 and Etna in 1971.

Tristan da Cunha is a lonely island in the middle of the South Atlantic ocean; before the workings of plate tectonics and continental

The active vent on Tristan da Cunha that forced the evacuation of 260 islanders in relief vessels like the one shown in the foreground.

A British naval officer looks at the island's steaming volcanic vent and one of the stone-and-thatch crofts threatened by the up-welling lava.

Evacuees on the shore.

and at the same time an object of such familiarity to the inhabitants of Sicily that it is treated with the contempt that (one is told) familiarity generally breeds – a tourist attraction, certainly, but not taken as a major threat to life and property.

This complacency, built up over 40 quiet years before 1971, was jolted by the harsh realities of life under the shadow of a major volcano by activity which began in April and persisted for more than six weeks. That the complacency was always unjustified is shown by the mountain's record of activity.

Crushed by colliding continents, Etna is basically a block of uplifted crust 30 miles (50 kilometers) across, from which various vents have spewed forth volcanic products over the millenia. The present cone lies in the debris of a collapse which followed a great eruption in 1669 which was the precursor of the more or less violent activity which has continued to the present day – 18 eruptions in the eighteenth century, 19 in the nineteenth, and five up to 1971 in the twentieth, including devastating eruptions in 1910 and 1928. The eruptions of 1971 began on 5 April when two cracks opened up below the summit of the present cone, throwing out bombs, ash and smoke,

while molten lava flowed down onto a flat plain below.

By a great stroke of irony, one of the first effects of the flow was to engulf a volcanological observatory built on the level plain by the University of Catania. Continuing its flow off the level and down slopes to the south, the lava flowed past a line of pylons carrying the ski lift, knocking them down in turn like a row of dominoes – hard luck for the scientists and skiers, but no great hazard, it seemed. Then on 6 May the nature of the eruption began to change completely.

On the afternoon of 7 May a great crack 0.6 miles (one kilometer) long, running eastward from the summit cone, became active from five large mouth-like fissures. The combined flow of lava from these five mouths reached 25 cubic yards (20 cubic meters) a second, showering lava down into the valley below. And then, on 12 May came the climax of the series of eruptions.

Yet another fissure now opened up, releasing lava from mouths along a 600-yard (550-meter) long front, which flowed down the mountain slopes to threaten the villages of Fornazzo and St Alfio. By now, of course, media interest in the eruption had been well and truly roused, and this dramatic new development was fully covered, appearing in

full color on TV screens not just in Europe but across the world. Forests and vineyards were destroyed by the flowing lava; a farmhouse was destroyed and the village of Fornazzo partially evacuated. But the main flow bypassed the village, cascading photogenically down into a dried up river bed. Although the village survived, roads were blocked and bridges cut by the advancing lava, and as other villages were threatened some observers suggested that the river of molten rock should be bombed in an attempt to divert its course.

This counsel of despair was ignored – and rightly so. For, if the lava had been bombed and then changed its path to engulf another village, the bombers would have had a lot of explaining to do to the villagers and their insurance companies. But happily no great damage was done by the flows, and the eruption ended, not with a whimper, but with a series of explosions producing plumes of dark ash, cauliflower shaped swirling clouds, and a rain of wet ash which blanketed the ground. By 28 May all was relatively quiet, and an explosion on 9 June which blasted a crater seven yards (six meters) across on the mountain slope was the final parting shot.

Later in the year Etna gave another rumble, erupting once again but still, fortunately for the inhabitants of Sicily, not disastrously. But the moral to be drawn is very clear. Judging by the history of the past three centuries, Etna is capable of doing a lot more than just disrupting the tourist industry for a season.

And Etna is not the only volcano in the area. To the north, in the Lipari Islands, there are several volcanoes including Stromboli and, of course, Vulcano itself; further north still, but on the same active line, is Vesuvius. The situation where continents collide is always more messy than at the clearcut lines of ocean ridges, or at the subduction zones where thin oceanic crust pushes under the thicker crust of continents. But, sooner or later, the Mediterranean is going to suffer another really big eruption, of the kind which destroyed Pompeii and, perhaps, Atlantis. Because of the very large population of the region today and the economic importance of its industry, this poses the greatest single volcanic threat to human society.

A wall of lava rolls inexorably across a Sicilian vineyard, May 1971. The two-month eruption, which produced only slow-moving lava and no destructive explosions, became something of an international TV spectacular.

Tempest Anderson (center) with two friends on a volcanic peak.

A *nuée ardente* from Mont Pelée similar to the one that destroyed St Pierre on 8 May 1902.

THE MARTINIQUE FIREBALL

In 1902 St Pierre, Martinique, basking in the warmth of tropical Caribbean waters, was called 'the Paris of the West Indies.' At 7.59 on the morning of 8 May, the town died when, with four deafening whiplash reports, Mount Pelée, six miles northeast of the city, burst apart. The explosions had been preceded by some volcanic activity which by hindsight might have offered some warning; but it was not sufficient. A *nuée ardente* or glowing cloud of superheated gases and incandescent particles exploded from the side of the mountain, swept downhill at 180 mph and annihilated the town and its 30,000 inhabitants as effectively as an atomic bomb. Within three minutes, St Pierre was reduced to a heap of burning rubble. There are, understandably, no photographs of the eruption itself, only of later displays and of effects of the eruption. These photographs, reproduced here for the first time, were taken shortly after the eruption by Tempest Anderson, a doctor from York, England, who had a passion for volcanoes – so much so that he returned five years later to record the way in which the island was recovering.

The rubble of St Pierre.

Looking out of the town towards the scorched hills.

Outside the town, there were eyewitnesses to the fireball, for the eruption had been building up for several days. When a hundred square yards (meters) of rock vaporized and the cloud licked as if from a giant flame-thrower towards St Pierre, one of them heard 'a continuous roar blending with staccato beats like the throbbing of a Gatling gun.' A crew member below deck in a ship in the harbor heard from above him 'weird inhuman sounds like the crying of seabirds in distress. I knew that up there people were being roasted to ashes.'

The first people to return to the stricken city were stupified by what they saw – wood turned to charcoal, iron bars twisted like pretzels, glass melted. One eyewitness wrote of a 'desert of desolation, encompassed by appalling silence . . . a world beyond the grave.' And a French scientist recoiled in horror from the 'pulverized, formless, putrid things which are all that is left of St Pierre.'

Amidst the ruins, masonry still perches crazily on rails and a visitor looks on, smoking his pipe, somewhat eccentrically, upsidedown.

A shattered villa.

Pelée erupted several times throughout 1902. Then its throat was sealed by a spine or plug of viscous lava which grew at the phenomenal rate of 30 feet (10 meters) per day to a total height of over a thousand feet above the crater rim. As it cooled, it tamped down the fires within. It has stayed solid ever since.

A close-up of the plug.

Inquisitive visitors at the still steaming crater.

By 1907 the blasted vegetation had begun to live again.

Five years later the slopes below Pelée were recovering.

The eruption early on the morning of the first day.

HEIMAEY'S SHROUD OF DEATH

Just before two in the morning on 23 January 1973, the clock on the main street of Heimaey, a few miles off Iceland's southern shores, stopped, shaken by an earth tremor. A few minutes later, fishermen out early saw the crust of the earth, east of the main volcanic cone of Helgafell, burst open.

It seemed doubtful whether they would ever see their homes again. Lava and ash poured out of the 1·2 miles (2 kilometer) vent, incinerating houses in its path and burying others ever more deeply. The 5000 inhabitants of the little town nestling at the foot of the new vent fled almost immediately in local fishing boats. No one was hurt and rescue teams came in to save what could be saved, shovelling ash off the roofs to prevent them collapsing before they were cleared. Windows were boarded up with corrugated iron to prevent the houses clogging with volcanic detritus.

It seemed doubtful if the householders would ever return, but at least the government was fighting for them. Heimaey produced some 17 percent of Iceland's fish exports and it was vital to the country's economy that the port be saved. A month after the eruption, workers established pipelines to the lava flow, enabling them to spray the molten rock with 500 tons of water per hour in an attempt to cool it and solidify it and thus allow it to build its own defense against the molten lava behind. It was the first time such a method had been used and the initial efforts were greeted with considerable skepticism.

The eruption as seen from the town.

Fighting a wall of lava with hoses.

Towards the end of February, an all out effort was made to save the harbor from closure by spraying the lava with 12,000 tons of water per hour from a patrolling ship. Together with the natural cooling effect of the sea, this operation was apparently successful.

By early March, water hoses had been deployed on the surface of the lava itself. In the third week of March, however, two rapid surges of lava engulfed the eastern section of the town, destroying another 70 houses. Nearly 25 percent of the town had been buried by lava. On 25 March, the lava, advancing now at walking pace, destroyed another 40 houses. Then, with ultimate perversity, the water cooling system broke down. New equipment rushed in from the United States enabled the flow to be resumed at the staggering rate of 200,000 tons per hour. Gradually, the lava flow abated and the town was saved.

Lava threatens to close the harbor.

Spraying the advancing lava.

A house explodes as the lava engulfs it.

In a surrealistic view, a house still standing supports a cone of ash.

The town threatened by the fissure of fire.

Notwithstanding this dismal view of part of the city in March, Heimaey did not die. After three months the eruption subsided. In July 1973 householders began to return. They found that the lava flow had actually improved the harbor. A year after the beginning of the eruption, life was returning to normal.

Laser beams streak out from a station set up by the University of Washington in Hollister, California to monitor earthquake activity on the San Andreas Fault.

6: THE FUTURE SHOCKS

The earth will be as active in the future as it has been in the past. Mountains will shift and explode, cliffs will fall, cities will be destroyed. In particular, California will continue to be torn apart along the San Andreas Fault. Our knowledge, however, will change – and with it, perhaps, our ability to predict and control earthquakes and volcanoes.

Slowly but surely the art of tectonic prediction is becoming a science; but in the late 1970s there is still an element of luck, as well as judgment, involved in the successful forecasting of either earthquakes or volcanic eruptions. For earthquakes, what is needed, of course, is the ability to forecast not only the location and time of major shakes but also their magnitude; various techniques have been developed.

The simplest of these techniques is the 'statistical' or probabilistic method, the basis, however deeply buried, of the size of the premiums charged for cover against such risks by the insurance companies. If earthquakes or eruptions occurred regularly, say every ten or 20 years, at a particular location this simple technique would be all that was needed. But things do not work out that way in practice. For example, the region of the San Andreas Fault is prone to large quakes – the northern stretch includes San Francisco, and the south includes Los Angeles. In the north, quakes occurred early in the nineteenth century and in 1906 while in the south history only goes back far enough to report a very big quake in the 1850s. There is a hint here that the critical regions suffer alternate disasters every 50 or 60 years, a hint which alone is enough to worry the inhabitants of Los Angeles and keep insurance premiums high. By such reckoning, the 'next' major quake in the Los Angeles region is overdue – but exactly when will it come? Here, one must turn to other techniques.

Perhaps the best prospect comes from studies of the way the pattern of local activity in the form of small earthquakes or the measured build-up of strain in the rocks changes in the years and months before an earthquake of major proportions. These effects are widespread and include: changes in the level of water in wells (squeezed by the changing pressure in the rocks); swarms of small earthquakes, or an ominous cessation of such activity altogether; changes in electrical properties of rocks due to changes in the water content; and changes in the local magnetic field, which may explain the stories of animals such as dogs and birds giving 'warning' of imminent earthquake disasters.

Where earthquakes produce these kinds of recognized precursor signs, prediction is already becoming a reality. And the best indicator of all, in terms of accurate forecasting of magnitude, time and location of earthquakes, is provided by the observations of changes in the speed with which shock waves move through the rocks in a region of earthquake risk – observations which are only possible using arrays of seismic detectors to monitor the changing activity, and are therefore, rather expensive. Still, it does work – at least some of the time.

This kind of study concentrates on two kinds of waves which are transmitted by the rock, the shear (S) waves and the pressure (P) waves, which travel by different processes involving different kinds of 'vibration' of the solid rock. Each kind of wave travels at its own characteristic velocity, and the ratio of these two velocities at a particular site at any time (P-velocity divided by S-velocity, say) turns out to be a guide to the state of strain in the rocks nearby.

Over the last ten years or so, studies in parts of the Soviet Union, in the United States and in Japan have all pointed in the same direction; this ratio of velocities changes by as much as 20 percent of its usual value in the period before an earthquake is due. The period over which this variation occurs can be as little as a few days for a small quake – magnitude 2 or 3 – or as much as five or six years for a major quake of magnitude 7, about a tenth as big as the 1906 disaster in San Francisco. Immediately before the quake, the seismic velocities return to 'normal,' giving the last minute warning of the onset of the disaster.

This is all very well as far as it goes, but to predict a real disaster one needs: the monitoring network in existence for six years or more; a constant small level of earthquake activity which produces shock waves whose velocity can be measured (or one needs to set off one's own explosive charges frequently, in order to produce man-made shock waves to monitor); and a co-operative earthquake which goes by these tentative rules, and does not 'do its thing' out of the blue, as, unfortunately, so many are prone to *without* producing the 'standard' velocity changes.

It might seem, though, that any help, however small, should be welcomed when it comes to earthquake prediction. Even if one can only say that a seismic velocity change which set in over a year ago suddenly stops, heralds the imminent arrival of a magnitude 6 earthquake, it ought to be a great advantage to modern society. But unfortunately that is still not the whole story. Geophysicists are not yet able to give 100 percent *certain* predictions in any case: the velocity changes could result from some other, outside cause; there might be a rogue earthquake which turns out to be bigger or smaller than the rule-of-thumb guide suggests; and so on. This raises the biggest problem of all in earthquake forecasting, the sociological, or moral question.

If there is any shadow of doubt at all, what is the best course of action? The first time an official agency forecasts a major quake in California, industry and individual life will be disrupted by precautionary measures. If the quake arrives as forecast, pats on the back will result all round. But the first time a forecast is wrong, and the quake does not appear on schedule, individuals and industry will be upset by the apparently needless disturbance of routine. A couple of such failures, and the next warning will be taken as an official crying 'wolf' and be ignored – and that might turn out to be the time that the quake is even worse than anticipated! This, in a nutshell, is the picture the administrators dread.

Less widely talked about is an equally grim alternative. If, for example, it is forecast that Los Angeles is due to be hit by a major quake in a week and it turns out to be correct, will the earthquake itself or the warning cause more overall damage? A panic reaction with congested highways, possibilities of looting, mob violence and fires in the deserted city, and the rundown of services – including, perhaps, hospital and fire-fighting services – during the days before the quake may make the total bill, in terms of lives and property, far greater than if no official warning had been issued, and if response to the situation had started on a big scale only after the disaster had hit. Callous though it may seem, the best kind of forecasts may be those which alert the disaster services to a high level of preparedness, but leave the ordinary citizen in the dark – but can this kind of forecasting ever be justified in our present western society?

Ironically, it is just in the present-day western society where it might be most acceptable to make this logical decision on the best course of action. In China where the role of the individual is clearly subservient to the needs of the State, a more general advance warning might be feasible. As the reaction to the severe earthquakes of 1976 in China showed, there as nowhere else in the world citizens respond calmly to disaster, carry out instructions from authority, and if necessary can evacuate entire teeming cities with the minimum of disruption.

For most, however the dilemma remains a cruel one. At present, the best course is to make sure that some kind of forecasting is available, at least to those in charge of disaster preparedness, with the harder decisions in the hands of the administrators – who must themselves be educated to be fully aware of this awesome responsibility.

Thus the most useful, practical forecast is, in many ways, just the kind now available –

The earth 50 million years hence, based on present-day plate movements. The Americas have shifted further westward. The San Andreas Fault has opened to let in the sea. Africa's Great Rift has done likewise. Australia has begun to collide with Asia.

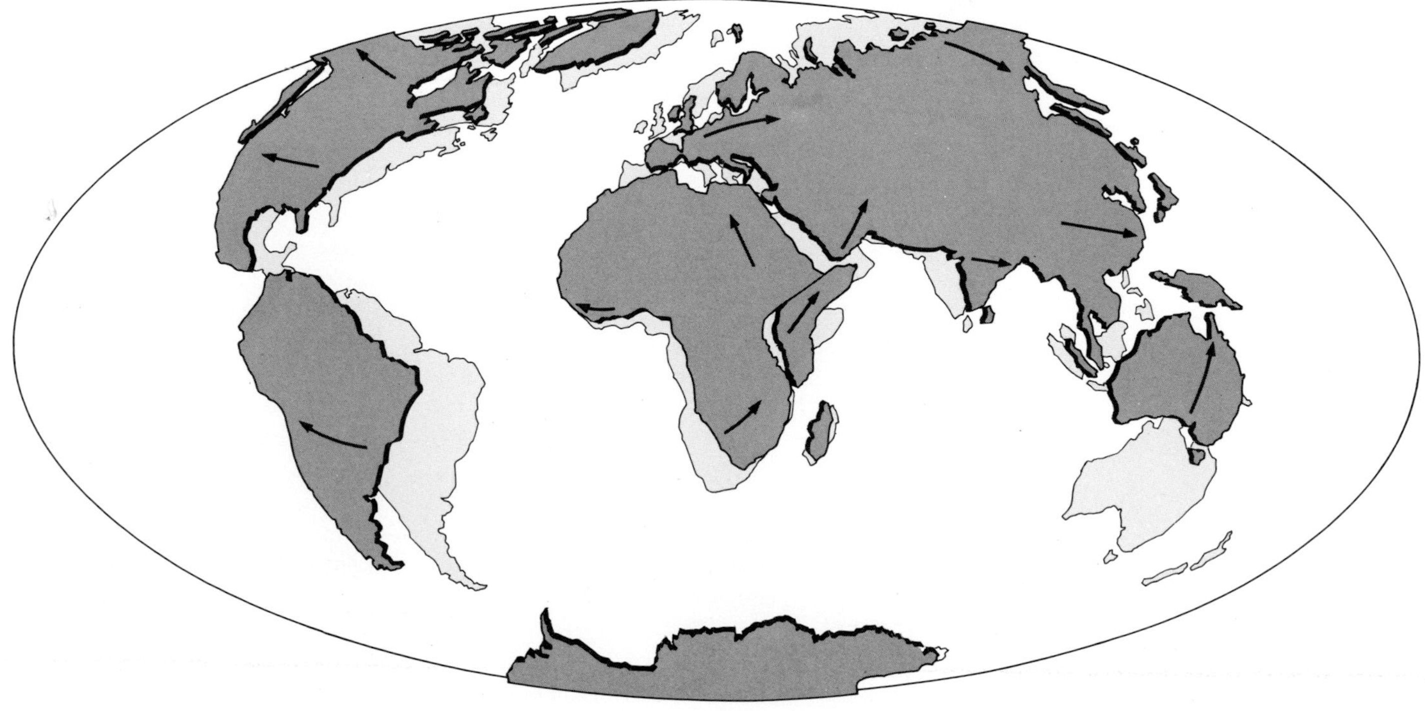

forecasts of increased risk of earthquakes in certain regions at certain times – periods of weeks, months or even a year or two. With this information, and a prepared disaster response, the effects can be minimized. And perhaps the sophistication of elaborate monitoring networks to study seismic velocity changes is not always necessary to make these broader forecasts of risk; major earthquake years, like 1976, may be forecast in advance so that responses at international level can be ready when the disasters strike, wherever in the world they actually hit. But this kind of broad forecasting inevitably includes volcanic as well as earthquake activity. Before one looks at the broad picture one should study the details of present day ability to forecast the occurrence and size of volcanic eruptions.

As with earthquakes, the forecasting of volcanoes can either be attempted on a statistical basis, trying to work out from past behavior just when a big volcano is next 'due' to erupt, or by monitoring changing conditions around the volcano to pick up precursors of major eruptions. The statistical method is better at giving a guide to relatively safe periods than at predicting specific eruptions, but even there the technique should be applied with caution and the results received with a degree of skepticism. After all, the concept deals with probabilities, not certainties. Even a 100 to one chance that a volcano might erupt could well be taken as disturbing, rather than reassuring.

However there are more direct methods of prediction. Here, the predictors ought to be much better off than earthquake predictors. The sites of the big volcanoes are well known, so there is no need for a very widespread net of observing instruments. Magma stirring in the bowels of a volcano prior to an eruption causes small but detectable changes in the local magnetic and gravitational fields. In addition, settling of material caused by the restless movement of magma can cause local earthquakes, or at a smaller scale, changes in the tilt of the mountain slope – again, small but quite measurable. Even without instru-

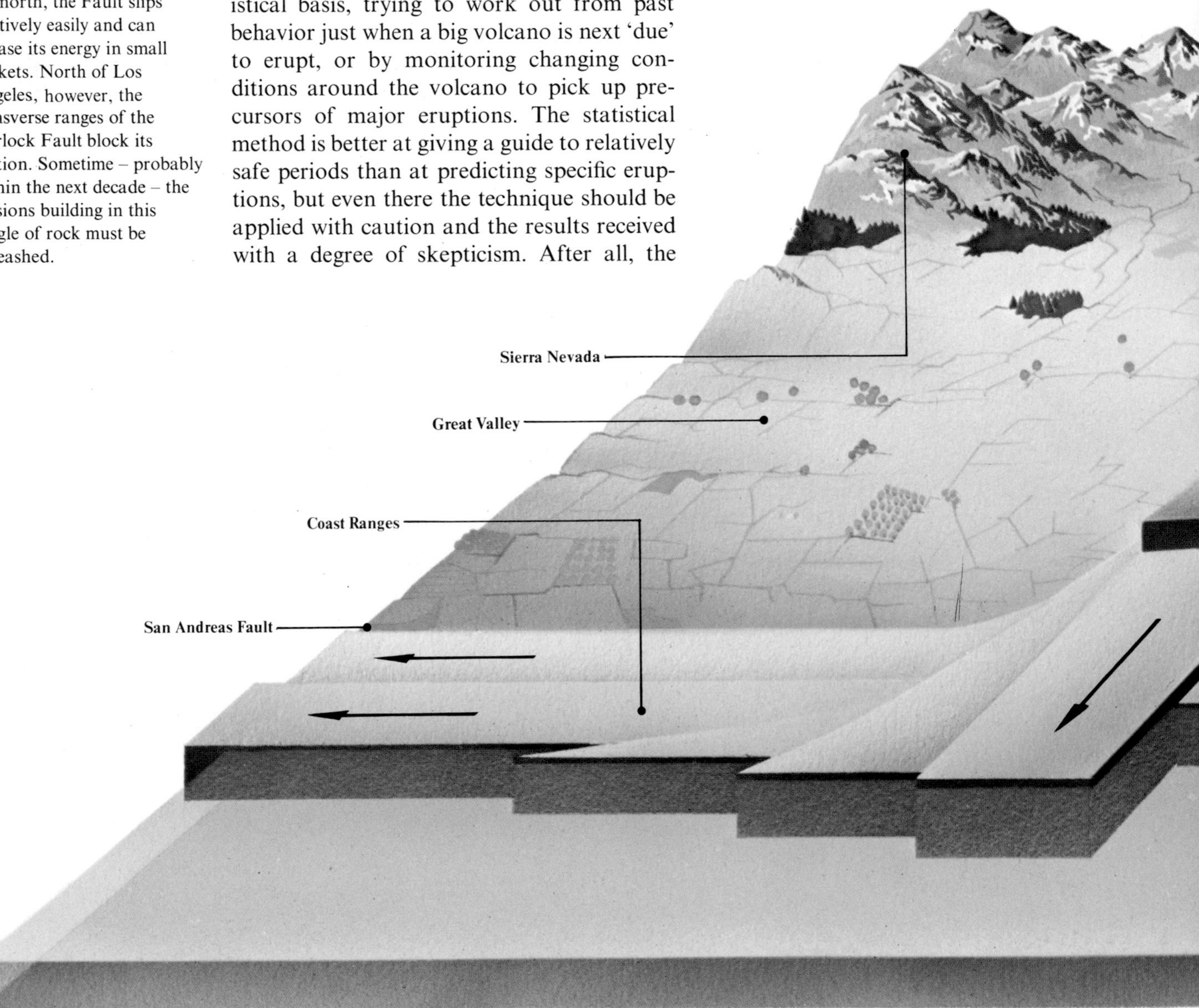

The complexities of the earth's crust around the southern section of the San Andreas Fault. On the ocean side of the Fault, land is moving northwards at the rate of about 1·5 to 2·5 inches (3·75–6·25 cm) per year. In the north, the Fault slips relatively easily and can release its energy in small packets. North of Los Angeles, however, the transverse ranges of the Garlock Fault block its motion. Sometime – probably within the next decade – the tensions building in this tangle of rock must be unleashed.

ments, the experienced volcano watcher can get early warning signs from changes in the production of smoke from the crater, and from the activity of nearby hot springs and geysers – a particularly sure indicator, one is told by those who live there, in the case of Vesuvius. The snag here, though, is that while each volcano may have its distinctive pattern of pre-eruption behavior, no two volcanoes necessarily behave in the same way, and only those observers who have lived with one, and watched it for many years are likely to pick out the particular nuances which signal the big eruption in each particular case.

Pessimists would say that the same applies to the more 'scientific' instrumental monitoring techniques, and it certainly is true that to predict the behavior of any one volcano means years of study of that volcano alone – generalities about the behavior of volcanoes are very hard to come by. Some volcanoes, for example, swell up measurably before an eruption as shown most dramatically by the 1943 eruption of Usu, in Japan, which was preceded by an upward doming of ground by as much as 45 yards (50 meters). Similar, though less extreme swelling has been observed before eruptions of Mauna Loa in Hawaii and Manam, north of New Guinea, among others; on the other hand many other volcanoes, such as Etna, show no such behavior, because the magma heart lies so deep that its pulsings do not affect the surface layers.

But success, when achieved, can be quite spectacular as forecasts go. Two Hawaiian examples make the point forcefully. In 1942,

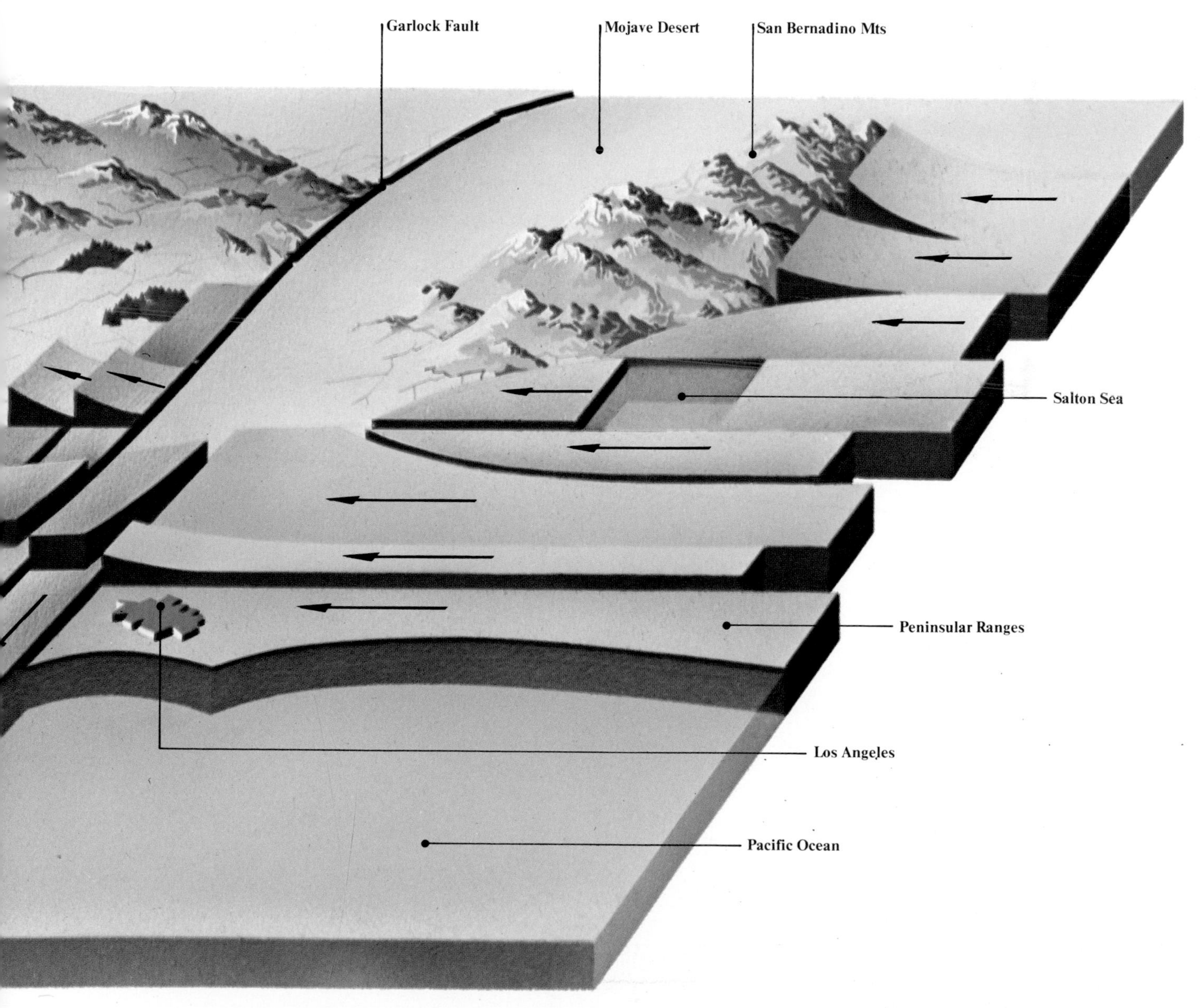

an earthquake on 8 February under the northeast flank of Mauna Loa was followed three and four days later by swarms of small, shallow earthquakes focused along a line running right under the volcano summit. In late March, further quakes and changes in the tilt showed observers that the volcano was being pumped full of magma, and a prediction was made that there would shortly be an eruption on the northeast rift zone, probably between 2970–3355 yards (2700–3050 meters) altitude. The eruption arrived on 28 April, at a height of 3080 yards (2800 meters).

Predictions combining various observations can also operate on much shorter time-scales. On 10 November 1973 at 5.30 in the afternoon, US Geological Survey observers on Kilauea in Hawaii noticed a seismological tremor coinciding with the draining of a small lava lake at the Mauna Ulu vent. Fifteen minutes later, a sudden and sharp change in tilt occurred; the overall pattern of events looked very much like the way things had gone before previous eruptions, and the Hawaii Volcanoes National Park Staff acted quickly to move more than 500 sightseers off the mountain. At 9.47 the same evening, an eruption from Mauna Ulu produced a flow of magma cutting both the mountain access road and the emergency escape roads – but by then, no visitors remained to be cut off by the fiery river of molten rock.

An equally valuable aspect of instrumental monitoring by tilt-meters and other devices is that they provide a clue about the end of a volcanic eruption. If a volcano is one of the kind that swells up before an eruption, then a flow of magma occurs and the crust settles down again; it may happen that the magma flow stops when the tilt is only part of the way

CHARLES RICHTER: THE FATHER OF EARTHQUAKE WATCHERS

The standard by which all earthquakes are measured is known as the Richter Scale, after Charles F Richter (right: center) of the California Institute of Technology, who devised it in 1935. The Richter Magnitude Scale measures the size of an earthquake at its source. The measurements are based on records made on a standard type of seismograph at a distance of 62 miles (100 km) from the epicenter. Seismographs from several different stations are normally used in computing the magnitude of a quake. Since stations are at varying distances from the source, records are compared and complex conversion tables are used to arrive at the final figure.

However, seismologists can make a fairly accurate estimate of magnitude within minutes after the earthquake from the record taken at only one seismographic station. It is this figure that newspapers usually report in their first stories about a quake. Magnitudes are expressed in whole numbers and decimals – usually between 3 and 8. However, these figures can be very misleading unless the mathematical basis for the Richter scale is understood. There are two important factors.

First, the maximum amplitude of earthquake waves recorded on the seismograph is transformed into a numerical figure by means of a logarithmic scale. This means that an increase of a whole number on the scale represents a *tenfold* increase in the size of the earthquake record. An earthquake of 8 magnitude is not twice that of a shock of 4 magnitude, but 10,000 times as great.

Second, the energy released at the source of earthquakes of different magnitudes is even more variable than the seismographic records they create. Again owing to the structure of the scale, an increase of one whole number indicates an energy release about 60 times greater than that of the next lower number. Therefore, a magnitude 8 earthquake generates about 10,000,000 times as much energy as a magnitude 4 shock.

The Richter Scale has no fixed maximum; however, observations have placed the largest known earthquakes in the world at the 8·8 or 8·9 level. The instrumental computation does not take into effect location or depth of hypocenter, or ground and structural conditions in the affected area. Richter numbers, therefore, cannot be used to estimate damage.

Damage may be indicated with another scale, named after a turn-of-the-century Italian seismologist, Mercalli. The 12-point Mercalli Scale relates the intensity of an earthquake to its effect on people and things. It ranges from a shock that causes slight dizziness and no damage to one that causes general panic, tosses objects into the air and destroys almost all buildings.

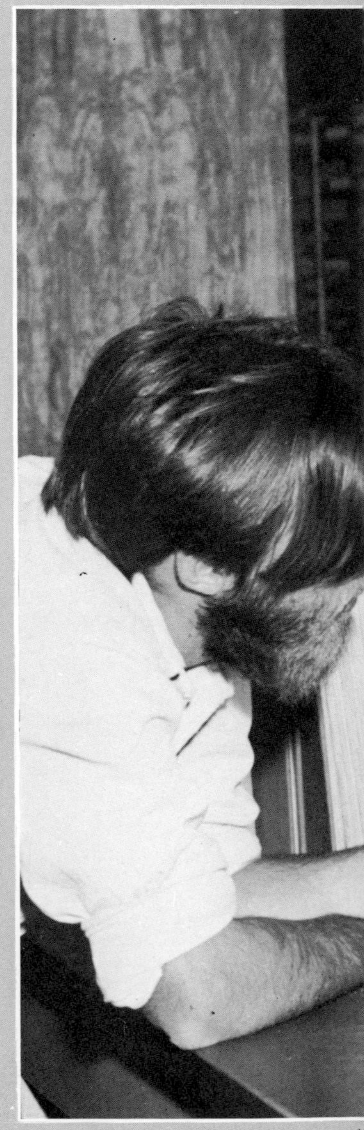

back to the original, pre-eruption conditions. The knowing volcanologist can take this as a sure sign that there is more magma inside the volcano ready to erupt. Clearly, the application of instrumental surveys and monitoring of volcanoes is at least one full step ahead of the state-of-the-art in earthquake prediction, and with this in mind it seems worth seriously considering an American proposal, reported in detail by Peter Francis, to apply space-age technology to the job.

The idea is based on the fact that there are only a few hundred really dangerous volcanoes around the world, a feasible number for continued monitoring. The technology that has enabled mankind to place automatic seismological stations on the Moon and Mars, relaying data back to Earth for analysis, is well up to the task of putting an automatic monitoring station on each of these dangerous volcanoes, with data relayed by telemetry up to a communications satellite in orbit around the Earth, then back to some central, manned, monitoring station at a research center on the ground. Such a control center, armed with an ever-improving array of information about the quirks and foibles of each individual volcano being watched, would certainly be able to provide warnings about many eruptions that would otherwise cause damage; the big snag, apart from cost, is that the one thing the system could *not* offer warnings about would be an unexpected eruption from a peak not thought to be volcanically active. And those eruptions are just the kind which are likely to cause the most damage, even though they are relatively rare.

That said, and with it always at the back of one's mind that the worst disasters are the unexpected, one can now step back from the

Soviet scientists study Krym Volcano in the Kurile Islands as a possible source of energy.

Mount Alaid in the Kurile Islands has also been considered as an energy source.

detail of specific forecasts to look at the broader, overall picture. If one has some idea of where and why earthquakes and volcanoes strike, and there is some broad understanding of when such violent processes are likely to be stirred up into more or less of a frenzy by natural forces, then one will be at least one step down the road to making sure that no such natural disaster ever takes the world *completely* by surprise.

Based on the modern plate tectonics version of the old idea of continental drift, the broad overview has already indicated which regions on the surface of the restless, shaking Earth are prone to tectonic activity of all kinds, and why. The gaps remaining in the broad overview are the how and when of major outbursts of activity, and it is by looking at the planet as a whole that these gaps are now being filled in.

Perhaps the single most important contribution to this aspect of the problem came from the continuing work of Professor Don Anderson, of California Institute of Technology, who gathered evidence that changes in the level of seismic activity from year to year and decade to decade correlate with the way the Earth's spin changes (with length of day edging up or down by a few thousandths of a second), and the way in which Earth's 'wobble' as it orbits the Sun also varies.

This whole field of study is as striking in its basic concepts as the theory of plate tectonics which affirms that solid rocks are subject to continual movement and rearrangement into new patterns; now, one is told that the whole of planet Earth, looked at in the large, is subject to twitches and tremors. Instead of sailing sedately through space in its grand orbit around the Sun, it actually staggers drunkenly around, spinning now faster, now slower and wobbling like an unstable spinning top. Of course, the graphic metaphors exaggerate the picture. The tremors, wobbles and spin are small in the same way that the movement of the continents is not something likely to knock one off his feet – except where

1983: A DATE TO REMEMBER

When will the next round of massive earthquakes strike? When, in particular, can Californians expect their next big shake? A number of possibilities are suggested in this chapter, but there is one particularly startling theory put forward by the author in his book *The Jupiter Effect*. He and his co-author Stephen Plagemann correlate earthquakes with sun-spot activity and the combined gravitational effects of the planets. In brief, their argument is as follows:

Between 1977 and 1984 the planets of the Solar System will be moving into an unusual pattern of alignments in which every planet is on the same side of the Sun, all occupying a narrow segment or 'pie-slice' of orbit and each aligning in turn with the others.

Such a pattern of alignments occurs only once every 179 years, and the slow build-up of the pattern may be related to an approximately 180-year rhythm in the pattern of the Sun's activity, which is revealed by – among other things – the changing number of dark spots seen on the face of the Sun.

These sun-spots reflect the strength of the solar wind, a stream of charged particles that 'blows' from the Sun, past the Earth and on into space. The 'wind' affects the Earth's magnetic field and atmosphere, helping to change the strength of atmospheric circulation and thereby giving a small but measurable shake to the spinning Earth. As the level of solar activity varies, so the solar wind blows strong or weak, steady or gusty.

If, then, the insistent tugging of the planets on the Sun plays a part in triggering solar activity – as now seems likely – the 1980's could prove literally an earthshattering decade.

To be more specific, studies of planetary motions show the greatest number of alignments (or conjunctions as they are known) of the kind linked by some observers with bursts of solar activity occurring between 1982 and 1984. Such a succession of conjunctions could lead in sequence to a peak of solar activity and a correspondingly gusty solar wind. Regions prone to tectonic activity could well be triggered in a 'last-straw' effect, providing a curious link between scientific forecasting and some of the astrological predictions of disaster linked with specific planetary alignments.

Certainly, dramatic effects have been expected from such auspicious events as long as man has studied the stars. Some astrologers mark the beginning of a new age by the occasion of the grand alignment – when Jupiter aligns with Mars and the Moon is in the Seventh House, the Age of Aquarius begins. The Age of Aquarius will be, we are told, a time of peace and love. But will it be ushered in by a major slip of the San Andreas Fault and a wave of earthquake activity?

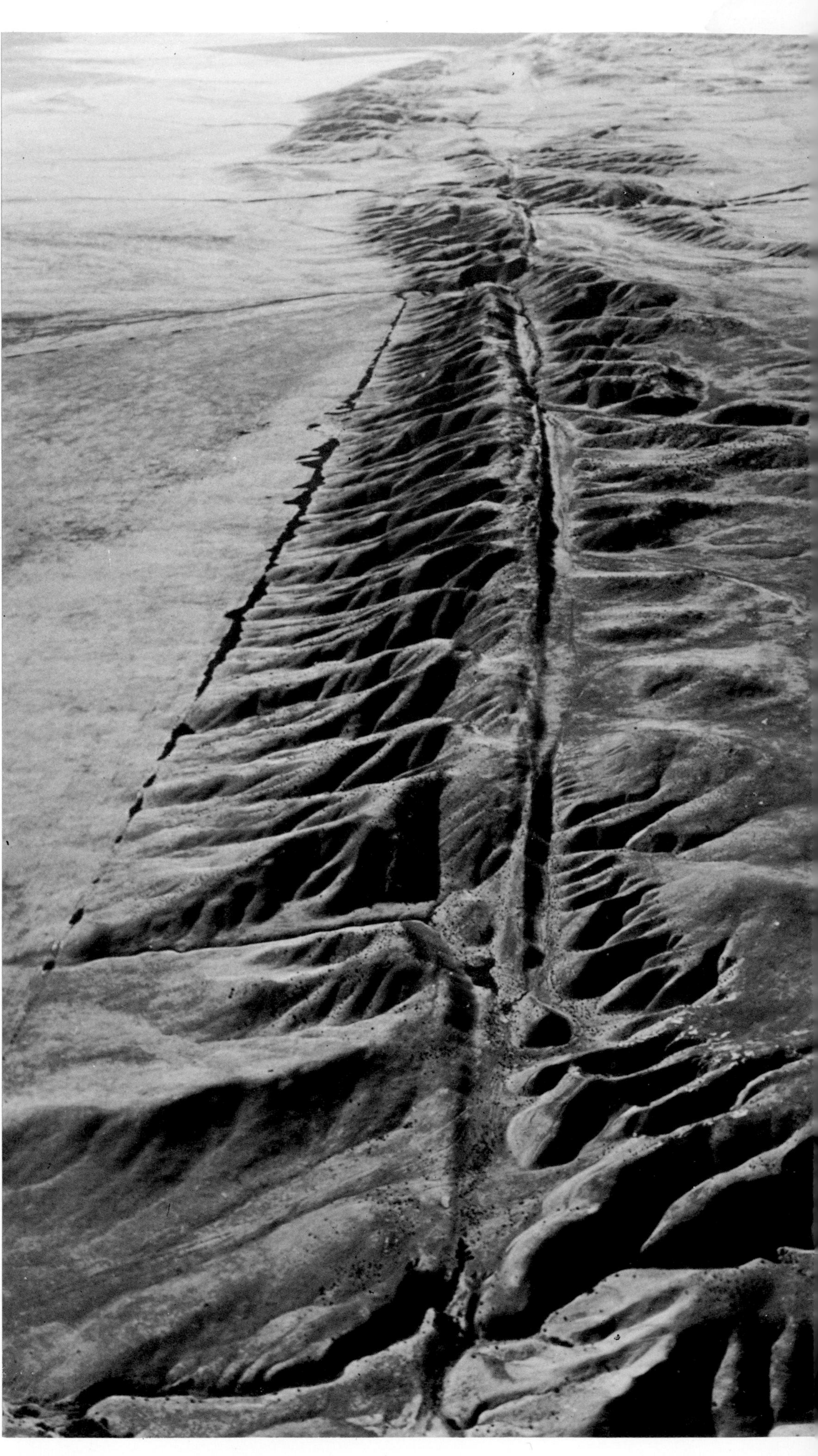

The San Andreas Fault as it slices across the Carrizo Plain about 40 miles (60 kilometers) inland and 100 miles (160 kilometers) north of Los Angeles. This is the most spectacular and desolate region of the Fault. Here the effects of regular movements between the two plates, their boundaries clearly marked by furrows and escarpments, are everywhere apparent. Land has been raised on one side or the other, then eroded. In many cases the erosion gullies have been offset by the movements of the plates to form small zig-zags.

Scientists on the San Andreas Fault at Hollister position a tilt-meter to monitor changes in alignment.

plate boundaries meet, and then only occasionally – but equally they are persistent and their effects are widespread. So they certainly cannot be ignored.

Shakes and wobbles in the spinning Earth's movements can now be measured very accurately by using atomic clocks to monitor the rate at which the stars appear to move across the sky, a rate which is due to the rotation of the Earth itself. But the larger wobbles can be picked out from records going back for decades using more traditional astronomical observations of the apparent variations in the position of the stars relative to the Earth's poles (in reality, changes in the direction the poles point relative to the essentially 'fixed' stars). The effect does not look too dramatic at first sight; the most significant of the 'wobbles' is a motion of the Earth's poles over an angle of less than half a second of arc taking about 14 months to complete a cycle. Named after the American, Seth Carlo Chandler, who measured it in 1891, this 'Chandler Wobble' can be put in perspective by comparing the small angle over which the nodding occurs with the apparent angular diameter of the Moon viewed from Earth – 30 *minutes* of arc, or half a degree, which with 60 seconds of arc in every minute makes the Chandler Wobble's angular variation equivalent to just one sixtieth of the Moon's angular diameter.

But shifting a whole planet about by even so small an amount means that a lot of energy, in human terms, is involved – indeed, it turns out to be just about the same amount of energy that is released in earthquakes around the globe over the same kind of period. And that coincidence has set a lot of geophysicists puzzling over causes and effects.

Don Anderson's studies of the available records have also looked at the changing length of day, which varies from decade to decade in a way which cannot be explained by simple astronomical theory – although again the effect is too small to justify resetting a watch to compensate, amounting to a few thousandths of a second compared with the 24 hours in the standard day. Relatively large changes in the length of day took place around the beginning of the twentieth century, just at a time when worldwide seismic activity was reaching a peak, including the San Francisco earthquake of 1906. Smaller, but still significant, peaks in the occurrence of earthquakes and in the plot of the changing length of day occurred in the 1830s and 1940s; and Anderson, among others, argues that this is no coincidence.

But which comes first? Does an outburst of seismic activity shake the Earth and affect its spin and wobble? Or does a jump in the spin shake up the Earth and jolt seismically active zones into life? Anderson ties cause and effect together in a neat, and plausible, feedback loop by bringing volcanoes into the scene.

In Chapter 4 it was noted how volcanic activity can affect the climate and weather through a direct influence on the circulation of the Earth's atmosphere. Explosive volcanic eruptions were more common in the nineteenth century than they have been so far in the twentieth, and Anderson suggests that this accounts, in large measure, for the changes in the length of day at the turn of the century. The argument is that the volcanoes affect the circulation of the whole atmosphere through the sunshield effects described in Chapter 4, and that the changing wind patterns affect the spin of the Earth.

This is in no way a far-fetched idea; Earth scientists know well that there is a seasonal change in the spin rate of the Earth caused by the seasonal shift of wind patterns from north to south, and the reason why the thin atmosphere can affect the fat Earth in this way is familiar to any ice skater. Those fancy spins in which skaters delight are adjusted by moving the skater's arms in and out; extend the arms, and spin slows (in line with the physical law of conservation of angular momentum); pull the arms in and the spin gets faster. It is because they are on the outside, farthest from the central axis of spin, that the arms are so important, even though their weight is much less than that of the body in the middle. And just the same effect works on an even more impressive scale, for the spinning-top, Earth.

The volcanic activity of the nineteenth century peaked in the 1830s and 1880s, the decades *before* changes in length of day and bursts of seismic activity. So the argument runs that volcanic outbursts come first, change the atmospheric circulation and weather, give a jolt to the spin of planet Earth, and thus trigger regions prone to earthquake activity into life. Because some parts of the globe are always in a state of tension – as the San Andreas Fault near Los Angeles is now – a small change in the rotation of the Earth will always set off earthquakes somewhere.

Just possibly, this overall pattern may be related to the seismic activity noticed in 1976, although really it is too early yet to be sure. In

A strain-meter in position in a mercury mine beneath Hollister set to record stress building in rock.

1977 Professor H Kanamori, a colleague of Anderson's at Cal Tech, made a survey of the statistics on energy released by earthquakes since 1900, looking in particular at the magnitudes of large earthquakes. Overall, the evidence shows that in recent years the Earth has been experiencing a period of relative calm, in earthquake terms, compared with the 1950s and 1960s.

However, looking at the Chandler Wobble indicator (rather than the length of day) Professor Kanamori notes that the size of the variation, though still small in absolute terms, grew from 1940 to 1950, stayed at a high level until the mid-1960s and has since declined. The temptation to link the recent burst of large-scale activity with the declining size of the Chandler Wobble is very strong; since the world's climate has been changing and moving into a new pattern of atmospheric circulation since the 1950s, one can even argue that the atmospheric changes have altered the wobble and thereby set off the earthquakes. The one thing that emerges ever more clearly from the continuing study of all the Earth sciences is the way the pieces fit together. Change the activity of the solid Earth and the weather is affected; change the weather, worldwide, and pay the price in earthquakes a decade later – sobering food for thought, perhaps, to the proponents of super-technology who envisage mankind one day controlling the weather at will.

But there is yet another aspect of this view of the workings of planet Earth as the parts of one machine, with many interlocking interactions. If something from outside the planet interfers with the Earth's workings then the effects will be felt in a variety of ways.

The only 'something' that could effectively do such a job is the Sun, which interacts with the Earth continuously through its outpouring of charged particles which stream past and become tangled in the Earth's magnetic field. This 'solar wind' of particles has only been investigated for ten years or so, since the space age got fully into its stride, and all its workings remain to be unraveled. One thing seems clear, however; when the Sun is more active, the wind blows stronger and 'gusty,' while when the Sun is quieter the wind dies away. In between times, the behavior is more steady.

Now, the Sun's pattern of behavior can be roughly understood and forecast in terms of the number of dark 'spots' that appear on its surface each year. At times of peak activity, many spots are present; when the Sun is quiet, the spots disappear. And the cycle over which this activity varies is about 11 years long, although it can be anything from nine to 13.

What does all this mean for the shaking Earth? In a nutshell, the years of minimum and maximum solar activity – the peaks and troughs of the 'sunspot cycle' – ought to be the years in which the Earth gets its biggest shaking from the solar wind. The peak years for obvious reasons will cause shaking – the wind then is buffeting and gusty. But the 'quiet' solar years also cause changes, since a sudden cessation of a gale can be just as unbalancing (as anyone who has tried walking into a strong wind will know) as an extra strong gust. In physical terms, it is always the change that unbalances a system, while steady pressure can usually be handled. And it makes very little difference whether the change is an increase or a decrease; it is the effects of a change in the balance that matters.

So, does the Earth show any signs of a jolt at these critical times? Overall, the evidence from studies of the length of day is clear, with roughly an 11-year-long ripple showing up in the records of the changing length of day on top of longer term trends. On specific occasions, the evidence is equally clear, and very large outbursts of solar activity in 1959 and 1972 have both been linked with specific jumps in the length of day by a few milliseconds when the blast from the resulting solar wind hit the Earth. And on the in-between scale, it now looks rather more than a coincidence that the most recent 'quiet Sun' year was 1976 – just the year in which a wave of large earthquakes brought a revival of widespread interest in the forces which shape the shaking Earth.

Records going back over past solar cycles show the same pattern – a noticeable increase in the occurrence of large earthquakes in the years around minimum or maximum solar activity. The year 1976, one might guess with hindsight, was particularly impressive in terms of large earthquakes because the wobble effect noted by Professor Kanamori was already starting to produce seismic repercussions when the solar cycle effect added its weight to the scales.

What does all this mean for the future shocks? It seems that humanity might well expect a burst of seismic activity around the globe, rivaling the headline-making activity of 1976 when the current solar cycle reaches its peak activity early in the 1980s. At that time, the plate boundaries prone to earthquakes

should get another shaking – places such as Japan, California, Alaska, the Middle East, and so on. Indeed, there is some reason to think that this next phase of solar shaking will disturb the Earth rather more than any other recent effect, because the Sun itself may be shaken into unusual activity by a rare alignment of the planets of the Solar System all tugging on the same side. But whether or not this possible extra influence operates as predicted, the ordinary increase in seismic activity at the time of solar maximum will still take place, which must be a sobering thought for any inhabitants of regions where earthquakes are known to occur but which have been relatively quiet, with no release of accumulating strain for the past few decades.

The obvious example of a region giving such cause for concern is Los Angeles, where, as has been stated earlier, there has been an interval of 120 years since the last major jolt of the southern part of the San Andreas. That means 120 years of accumulated plate movement to be released next time there is a jolt – rather more earthquake energy than that liberated in the 1906 disaster further north in San Francisco. It is difficult to see any way in which such an extreme situation can be eased without a disaster. But there is hope that after this inevitable next big California earthquake this kind of seismic shock may be brought under control.

In outline, the idea is simple. Where two tectonic plates rub past one another, as in California, the greatest earthquake damage occurs when, as in San Francisco or Los Angeles, the movement is jerky. One earthquake every 100 or 150 years means one disaster every 100 or 150 years. But 100 or 1000 earthquakes every 100 years would be a quite different story, provided they released the same amount of strain over the entire period. This is just what happens in the central part of the San Andreas system, where continual 'creep' allows the Pacific and North American plates to inch past one another without disturbing life on the surface of the Earth – except for the inconvenience caused where badly planned roads, fences or water pipes cross the creep zone and are slowly bent and distorted by the creep.

If the entire San Andreas could be encouraged to creep more or less smoothly, instead of moving in fits and starts, the earthquake hazard in California would be greatly reduced. The job could almost certainly be done, by drilling boreholes into the fault regions which are presently 'locked' and pumping water down to lubricate them. But the problem is that if that is done today the lubrication is likely to release all that 120 years' accumulated strain mentioned above (or 70 years' strain if tried in the northern region). So the only real hope of achieving success with this kind of control is to let nature take its course and produce the big crunch, perhaps in the early 1980s, and *then* to pick up the pieces and try to encourage smoother movement of the sticky parts of the fault in future.

Not much comfort to the present inhabitants of Los Angeles! And not much comfort from this technique for anyone else, either, since it can only work where plates slide past one another. Earthquakes produced where plates collide (such as the Middle East) or where oceanic crust is being destroyed by a deep trench (such as the region near Japan) will never be tamed in this way. Earthquake *control*, it seems, is a lot further off than some form of reliable earthquake *prediction*. The future shocks are going to come anyway, and the world must learn how best to cope with them rather than fostering any grandiose schemes to change the geophysical environment to suit mankind.

Daly City, just south of San Francisco, straddles the San Andreas Fault and is at high risk when the next shake comes.

BIBLIOGRAPHY

David Dinely, *Earth's Voyage Through Time* (Paladin, London, 1973).
A comprehensive and readable guide from the viewpoint of a geologist.

John Gribbin, *Our Changing Planet* (Wildwood, London & Crowell, New York, 1977).
Sets our shaking Earth in its perspective as a small planet.

John Gribbin & Stephen Plagemann, *The Jupiter Effect* (Fontana, London, 1977; Vintage, New York, revised edition 1976).
More about the San Andreas Fault and a prediction of the next major California earthquake.

Peter J. Smith, *Topics in Geophysics* (Open University Press, Bletchley, 1973).
The best short introduction to serious geophysics for the student or reader with some scientific knowledge.

Peter Francis, *Volcanoes* (Penguin, 1976).
The only detailed, comprehensive account I know of which is also readable. Although a fairly hefty 350+ pages, and not exactly light bedtime reading, this is the best place to begin if you want to know more about the subject.

Geological Museum, London, *Volcanoes*.
A pamphlet of breathtaking pictures and diagrams, plus a few well chosen words of explanation.

John Gribbin, *The Climatic Threat* (Fontana, 1978).
A perspective on climatic change, and especially current changes as they are affecting mankind, from the viewpoint of an astronomer but with some discussion of the role played by volcanoes.

ACKNOWLEDGEMENTS

Acme Photo (Charles Seawood): 128–9.
Associated Press Ltd: 43.
Atkins: 45, 109 middle, 163 right, 166 bottom.
Laurence Bradbury: 60–1, 132–3.
Bruce Coleman Ltd: 48 bottom (A.J. Deane), 50 (David Goulston), 50–1 (David Goulston), 52–3 (Lee Lyon), 53 inset (Lee Lyon), 54–5 (Goetz D. Plage), 113 (Fritz Prenzel), 130–1 (Werner Stoy), 139 (Werner Stoy).
California Historical Society Library: 89, 94–5.
California Palace of the Legion of Honour: back cover.
Culver Pictures Inc: Title page, 68, 69, 88–9, 90–1, 92 bottom.
Diagram: 48, 100.
P.W. Francis: 8, 9, 46 top and bottom, 104, 105, 108 top, middle and bottom, 109 top, 116 top, 117 top, 122.
The Geological Museum, London: Front cover, 38, 143 top left (J.E. Guest), 162–3.
Peter Griffiths: 12–13, 14, 15.
John E. Guest: 148–9.
Gary Hinks: 36–7, 40–1, 44, 58–9, 102–3, 110, 173, 174–5.
Institute of Geological Sciences: 106.
Keystone Press Agency: 23 bottom, 24 bottom, 26–7, 73, 74–5 top, 75 top, 76–7, 164–5, 165 top and bottom, 178 top and bottom.
Liaison Agency: 22, 70–1.
Manchester Guardian: 147 left.
Mary Evans Picture Library: Endpaper, 6–7, 10–11, 16, 18, 30–1, 136, 137 bottom, 148 inset.
Marion Morrison: 109 bottom, 117 bottom.
Tony Morrison: 111, 116 bottom.
National Aeronautics and Space Administration (NASA), Washington DC: 28–9, 33, 112.
Chuck O'Rear: 170–1, 182, 184, 186.
Oxford Museum: 120–1, 124–5.
Picturepoint Ltd: 106–7, 121, 122–3, 128 top, 140 top and bottom, 143 top right, 143 bottom.
Popperfoto: 17, 23 top, 72, 74 left, 74–5 bottom, 80, 82, 145, 146 inset, 147 right.
Pronda Pronda: 127 top.
Radio Times Hulton Picture Library: 10, 32, 64–5, 65, 66–7, 92 top, 93 top, 126 top, 126–7, 137 top, 141.
Susan Griggs Agency: 134–5 (Adam Woolfit), 135 top and bottom, 142 top and bottom (Ivan Polunin). Sygma 4–5, 20–1, 21, 24 top, 25, 56–7, 78 top, 78–9, 79, 83, 84–5, 86, 150–1, 168–9.
Susan Goldblatt: Index
H. Tassiel: 98–9.
U.S. Geological Survey: 81, 177, 180, 181 top and bottom.
United Press International Photo: 146.
Wells Fargo Bank: 92–3, 94 top, 96–7.
York Museum, Tempest Anderson Collection: 127, 152–61.
Zefa: 62 (W. Janoud), 63 (W. Janoud), 138–9 (W. Stoy), 140 bottom (Ray Halin), 166 top, 166–7.
Thanks are also due to the Geological Museum, London for supplying diagramatic material.

INDEX

Abberton *17*
Agadir earthquake, Morocco 1960 11, 61, 82, *82*
Akrotiri 135
Alaid mountain, Kurile Islands *178*
Ambato cathedral, Ecuador *15*
Anak Krakatoa 141, *142*
Anchorage earthquake, Alaska 1964 61, *80*, 80–1, *81*
Anderson, Professor Don 179, 183, 185
Anderson, Tempest *152*, 153
Arenal, Costa Rica *105*, *108*
Arica earthquake, Peru 1868 *68*
Aristotle 32
Atacama Desert, Chile *117*
Atlantis legend 8, 135, 148, 151
Atlantis II Deep 42
Aucanquilcha volcano, Chile *46*

Bacon, Francis 30
'Bombs' of lava *104*, 105, 149
Brendan, Saint 12–13
Bryan, Eliza 13
Bucharest earthquake, Rumania 1975 *57*, 61
Buckland, William 121
Bullard, Sir Edward 32, 34

Caldiran earthquake, Turkey 1976 61, *78–9*
California Institute of Technology 176, 179, 185
Candide (Voltaire) 19
Carrizo Plain *180–1*
Cerro Rici Volcano, Bolivia *46*, 47
Chandler, Seth Carlo 183
'Chandler Wobble' 183, 185
Chase, Thomas 19, 69–76, 87
China Reconstructs 9
Cotopaxi, Ecuador *117*
Ciparis, Auguste 144, 145
Climatic development and effects 104, 105, 112–19, 132, 141
Colgate, Dr S A 188
Colchester 17
Compère-Leandre, Léon 145
Continental drift theory 28–31, 32, 34–5, 36, 38–9, 68, 100, 145, 179, *see also* Plate tectonics theory
Cook, Police Sergeant Jesse 89
Comstock Lode, Nevada 47
Crete 135
Cripple Creek, Colorado 47
Culham Research Laboratory 188

Daly City *187*
Death toll 8, 10, 12, 19, 20, 21, 24, 58, 61, 62, 65, 68, 69, 72, 77, 79, 82, 107, 108, 133, 141
Deepsea Miner II 45
Disasters *see under individual place names*
'Dust Veil Index' 117, 118, 119

Earth, formation of 28–55, *30–1*, *33*, *36–7*, *173*
Earthquake (film) 58
Earthquakes: control of *163*, *165*, 187; effects of 58–9, *see also* Fire, Floods explanation of *see* Plate tectonics theory; man-made 188; prediction 9, 32, 171–87; timing of 79–80; *see also under individual place names*
Ecuador earthquake *see* Peru and Ecuador earthquake 1866
El Misti, Peru *109*
Erebus mountain 103
Erzincan earthquake, Turkey 1939 61
Etna mountain 9, *26*, 49, *98*, 103, *104*, 133, 145, *148*, *149*, 148–51, *151*, 175
Evelyn, John 118

FCIs (fuel coolant interactions) 188
Falling Mountain 16
Fire 58, 59, 60–2, 65, 73, 80, 88, 89
Floods 58, 77
Forg, John 19
Francis, Peter (*Volcanoes*) 47, 49, 177
Fuego 133
Fuji 133

Galapagos Rift 42, 43
'Gang of Four' 11
Gemona earthquake, Italy 1976 23, 61, *70–1*
Genthe, Arnold 91
Glomar Explorer 43, 43–5
Golden Gate Park (tent city) 92, *92*, *93*
Great Fire of London 1666 95
Great Rift Valley *see* Rift Valley
Gregory, John Walter 50
Gregory Rift *see* Rift Valley
Guatemala City earthquake 1976 *24*, *25*, 61, 82–7; *83*, *84*, *86*
Guatemala National Observatory 57

Hawaii 39, 40, 41, 101, 102, 109, 112, *131*, 139, *140*, 175
Hawaiian eruptions 102, *102*, 144
Heimaey, Iceland 133, *162–9*, 188
Hekla eruption, Iceland *107*
Helgafell, Iceland *162*, *163*
Hiroshima 8, 105
Hollister 182, 184
Honjo Clothing Depot 65
'Hot Spots' 40, 101, 139
Hughes, Howard 43, 45

Ice Ages 115, 116, 117, 118, 119
Iceland 12–13, 39, *45*, 49, 101, 102, *109*, 118, 142, 143–4, 148, 188, *see also under individual place names*

Japan 39, 40, 101, 118, *see also under individual place names*
'Jigsaw puzzle' evidence of earth movement *see theories of* Continental Drift *and* Plate tectonics

Kanamori, Professor H 185
Kansu earthquake, China 1920 61
Katmai eruption, Alaska 1912 15–16, 133
Kelut 133
Kilauea *131*, 133, *138*, *139*, 139–40, 176
Kirkjufell (Heimaey) 133
Krakatoa 14, 103, 104, 116, 118, 119, 132, 133–41, *136*, *141*, *142*, 144, 188

La Soufrière 119
Lake Naivasha, Kenya *48*
Lake Van earthquake, Turkey 1976 *20*
Lamb, Professor Hubert 115, 117, 118, 119
Land bridge theory 31–2, 34
Laser beams *170*
Lava *108–9*, 109 *see also* Bombs
Lisbon earthquake, Portugal 1755 *7*, *18*, 19, 61, 68–77, 87
Los Alamos Scientific Laboratory, New Mexico 49
Los Angeles earthquake 1971 61, 77
Lower Van Norman Lake 77

McCullen, Captain C B (of *Dora*) 15
Magma 35, 39, 47, 54, 100, 101, 110
Malha, Sudan *116*
Managua earthquake, Nicaragua 1972 61
Manam 175
Mao Tse-tung, Chairman 9
Mariner 9 space probe 112
Mars 109, *112*, 112–14, 177, 179

Mass, Dr Clifford 119
Mauna Loa, Hawaii 109, 133, 175
Mauna Ulu 176
Melville (research vessel) 42
Messina earthquake, Nicaragua 1972 61
Mid-Atlantic Ridge 42, *44*, 46, 144, 147
Mining: copper 47; diamonds 47–9; gold 47; manganese 42–3; sea and sea-bed 42–5; silver 46, 47; sulphur 46, 49; *see also* Resources of the earth
Mitchell, John 68
Mountains *see under individual names*

National Geographic 84
Neale, Reverend Philip 137
Nevado de Sajama, Bolivian Andes *116*
New Madrid earthquake, Missouri 1811 13, 61
Ngong Hills, Kenya *50–1*
Nguruman Scarp 50
Niigata earthquake, Japan 1964 61, *74–5*
Novarupta 16
Nuées ardentes 105–7, 108, 117, *152*, 153
Nyirangongo volcano, Zaire *54–5*

Ocean ridges 38–9, 101, 102, *see also* Mid-Atlantic Ridge
Ocean trenches (deeps) *39*, 40, 42, 100–1
Ol Doinyo Lengai (Mountain of God) *53*, 133
Orloff, Ivan 16
Oxford Museum 121

Paleomagnetic studies 35–8
Panama-Pacific International Exposition 95
Pangaea 36, 50
Paricutin 133
Peking 9–11, *10*; temporary tent housing *10*, *12*
Pelée mountain 106–8, 116, 119, 133, 144, 152, 153, *158–61*
Peléean eruptions *103*, 106, 108
Perry, Captain K W (of *Manning*) 16
Peru and Ecuador earthquake 1866 61
Planetary movements 112, 179
Plate tectonics theory 32–5, 38, 40–1, *40–1*, 42, 43, 46, 68, 100, 135, 145, 148, 179, *see also theory of* Continental Drift
Plato 135
Plinian eruptions *103*, 106, 108
Pliny the Elder 104, 122
Pliny the Younger 104, 121, 122–3
Pompeii 103, 104, 108, 121, *121*, 122, *122*, *123*, 148, 151
Pumice 108, 117, 133, 143

Quetta earthquake, Pakistan 1935 61

Resources of the earth: geothermal power 49, 178; oil 46–7, 49; *see also* Mining
Richter, Charles F 176, *177*
Richter Scale 59, 74, 82, 176
Rift Valley *48*, 50, 101, 173
'Ring of Fire' 15, 40, 100, 132

St Pierre, Martinique 106–8, 144–5, 152, 153, *154–7*, 157
Sakurajima earthquake, Japan 1914 11–12
San Andreas Fault 39, 40, 60, 82, 170, 171, 173, 174, 179, *180–1*, 182, 187
San Fernando Valley, California *77*
San Francisco earthquake 1906 13, 39, 58–60, 61, 69, 82, 88–95, *88–96*, 132, 172, 183, 187
Satellite photographs: Africa, Asia *28*; Persian Gulf *32*
Schmitz, Eugene, Mayor of San Francisco 91
Schneider, Dr Stephen 119
Scripps Institution 43
Seneca 121
Shanshi province earthquake, China 1556 8
Shield volcanoes 109, 112, 144
Sigurgeirsson, Dr Thorbjörn 188
Skitaretz, Petroff 62
Skopje earthquake, Yugoslavia 1963 23, 61, 72, *72–3*
Snider, Antonio 30
Société Astronomique de France 145
'Solar wind' 179, 185
Somma mountain 104, 121
Stromboli 9, 103, *113*, 133, 151
Strombolian eruptions *102*, 103
Sun's effect on earth *114*, 116, 185–7
Surtsey, Iceland 133, 142, *143*, 143–4, 147

Taal 133
Tacitus 122
Tambora eruption 1815 105, 133
Tangshan earthquake, China 1976 8–9, 10, 61
Tenerife *108*, *109*
Thera (Thira) 8, 133, *134*, *135*
Tidal waves (tsunami) 7, 61, 65, 68, *68*, 81, 82, 132, 135, 137, 141
Tokyo earthquake, Japan 1923 11, 60–3, 65, *66–7*, 74
Tristan da Cunha 133, *145*, 145–7, *146–7*, 148
Tsunami *see* Tidal waves
Turkey earthquake 1966 *24*
Tuscania earthquake 1971 *23*

Union Minière Company, Belgium 45
Universities of: Cambridge 32; Catania 150; East Anglia 115; Hawaii 49; Washington 170
Urrutia, Don Claudio 87
Usu, Japan 175

Valley of Ten Thousand Smokes 16
Vesuvian eruptions 103, *103*, 106
Vesuvius 9, 49, 103–4, 120–1, *120*, 122, *123–9*, 133, 140, 151, 175
Viking space probe 112
Volcanoes: classification of eruptions 100–4; location of 100–1; products of 105, 108–9, 110, *see also* 'Bombs', Lava; structure and workings of 99–129; *see also under individual names*
Volcanoes National Park, Hawaii *140*, 176
Vulcanian eruptions *102*, 103, 106–7, 108
Vulcano *9*, 103, 133, 151

Wade, Nigel 9–11
Wegener, Alfred 30, 31, 32, 34
Western Rift 50, 54
Westman Islands 142, 143
Witwatersrand gold-field, South Africa 47

Yokohama earthquake, Japan 1923 *see* Tokyo earthquake
Yungay earthquake, Peru 1970 61